THE FIVE
MONEY
PERSONALITIES

Speaking the Same
LOVE and MONEY Language

TAYLOR & MEGAN KOVAR

W PUBLISHING GROUP

AN IMPRINT OF THOMAS NELSON

The Five Money Personalities

© 2023 Taylor & Megan Kovar

Published in Nashville, Tennessee, by W Publishing, an imprint of Thomas Nelson.

Thomas Nelson titles may be purchased in bulk for educational, business, fundraising, or sales promotional use. For information, please email SpecialMarkets@ThomasNelson.com.

Any internet addresses, phone numbers, or company or product information printed in this book are offered as a resource and are not intended in any way to be or to imply an endorsement by Thomas Nelson, nor does Thomas Nelson vouch for the existence, content, or services of these sites, phone numbers, companies, or products beyond the life of this book.

ISBN 978-1-4003-4020-0 (audiobook)
ISBN 978-1-4003-4019-4 (eBook)
ISBN 978-1-4003-4018-7 (TP)

Library of Congress Control Number: 2023935191

Printed in the United States of America
23 24 25 26 27 LBC 5 4 3 2 1

We dedicate this book to our children.
They are the why behind everything we do.
We love you.

CONTENTS

CONTENTS

INTRODUCTION

IN 2004 I (Taylor) decided to do something bold. A 2005 Mustang had just arrived on the lot of a local dealership, and it was the only car of its kind in town. I was eighteen and working at a plywood mill, making enough money to get by but definitely not enough to buy a new car. The thought of owning anything other than a used beater had never entered my mind.

Until I saw that 'Stang. She called to me. I had to have her.

Driving off the lot I felt like a million bucks. Everywhere I went people would stop and stare as I drove past. When I parked at the store or the movie theater, strangers would tell me how nice my car was.

A custom "KOVAR" license plate let everyone know just who the baller in the gray Mustang was. I knew what they were thinking when they watched me cruise down Main Street: "There goes Taylor Kovar. He's the man."

Everyone was impressed; everyone was jealous; everyone

knew I was on the rise. But as nice as it was to get all the smiles and thumbs up from my buddies, there was only one person I wanted to impress. When I signed the last page of that contract and those keys landed in my palm, I was only thinking about one lady's praise: the future Mrs. Kovar.

Driving over to Megan's house in my brand-new ride, I knew she was going to lose her mind. She wouldn't be able to believe how blessed she was, dating such a high roller.

She saw me roll up, and just as I'd expected, she was speechless.

Unfortunately, it was for all the wrong reasons.

You've never seen a baller deflate so quickly. No high roller has ever fallen so low. No man has ever so quickly become *not* the man.

Buying that car was the dumbest thing I could have done.

Megan didn't have to say much to convince me of this— she had the facts on her side. Never mind that my father had to cosign on the loan, even after trying to talk me out of it. Never mind that the $22,000 it cost me was about $20,000 more than I had. Never mind that I was working the graveyard shift at the mill and the last thing I needed was a flashy car to get me to and from work.

The thing was a disaster on wheels.

Here's some truth: it doesn't matter how pretty your car is if the gas tank doesn't work. Most of the time I could only get about half a tank before the pump would register the car as full and stop me from fueling it up all the way. Then I'd burn through the half tank in about five minutes, and I'd be right back at the gas station.

The beautiful gray interior, the one I loved so much during the test drive, couldn't avoid stains to save its life. Even drops of water left marks. A month into ownership and the seat covers were already unsalvageable.

So there I was, thousands of dollars in debt, driving a stained-up Mustang with a perpetually empty tank, hoping my high school sweetheart would look past my mistake and still decide to marry me.

Spoiler alert: she did.

All these years later, Megan and I are married with a beautiful family and an incredible life together. In the grand scheme of things, that idiotic purchase was just a tiny drop in the bucket. At the same time, that one decision could have been the end of us. That impulsive move could have sent Megan running for the hills, and no one would have blamed her. Or she could have stayed with me and blamed all our money troubles on the time I bought a car I had no business buying. It's easy to imagine that one purchase could have wrecked our relationship because the subsequent fights about money almost tore us apart.

What helped us move on wasn't a sudden windfall or a

car crash and an insurance payout. Even while dealing with debt, Megan and I made a conscious effort to better understand each other's—and our own—perspectives on money. There was no question about whether I had made the wrong move buying that car, but Megan took the time to understand what motivated me to do it. Instead of brushing off her concern about my hefty loan, I learned why debt gave her so much more anxiety than it gave me.

In the end it wasn't about the money; it was about each other and our communication. We still have very different tendencies when it comes to finance, and money fights still happen from time to time. Fortunately, we've come a long way since that meltdown in 2004, and we know how to work through our issues with clear heads and compassion.

And now we're excited to pass the knowledge and experience we've gained on to other couples looking to make things a little better.

This journey toward a strong Money Relationship can feel like a long haul, but if you're committed to finding strength in each other along the way, you can *Make It Happen*. By picking up this book, you've already made the decision to strengthen your relationship and dream about the future. It won't happen overnight, and it won't happen without both of you deciding you want to start fresh and build a great life together. But if you're determined, you can *Make It Happen*. We've seen it with hundreds of couples, and we've seen it in our own relationship.

The Big Picture

Before you jump in, we want to be clear about something: this book is not a guide on how to manage your money. You won't find tricks for creating a balanced budget or tips on saving money. We aren't going to teach you how to find the best investments or how to reduce your mortgage. There are plenty of books out there that do all of that, and more.

This book is about you and your marriage. It's about the way your money and your relationship combine to create a Money Relationship. That's right, you and your spouse have a Money Relationship, just like you have an emotional relationship and a spiritual relationship and a physical relationship.

Every couple recognizes those times when they are emotionally out of sync. One of you is upset, and the other person can't understand why. Many of us know how it feels to be at a different place than our spouse when it comes to faith. All of us have had those nights where one of us is in the mood to stay up late and the other just needs to go to sleep.

Your Money Relationship is no different. When you and your spouse are making financial decisions—the big ones and the little ones—there will be times when you completely get each other, when you make a plan to spend or save or invest and you head down that financial road together. If you're like nearly every couple we've ever met, there are other times when your love and your money turn into a toxic mess. You can't agree on a plan or you can't stick to the plans you've made or you just can't understand why your spouse doesn't see things the way you do. Like every other aspect of your relationship, the money piece can either help you grow closer or pull you apart.

We believe that when couples have the right tools and are committed to using them, they can make their love and their money work together to create a thriving Money Relationship and an intimate, solid marriage.

Why Your Money Relationship Matters

Taylor has years and years of experience with financial planning, and together we have the mutual experience of overcoming money issues within our own relationship. Even with that collective knowledge, he and I (Megan) both spent a long time assuming married couples could have a strong financial future with a clear budget and a healthy savings account. We've learned how wrong that assumption was—in our personal life, in the marriages of Taylor's clients, and with the couples he and I have advised together.

A lot of our education came from none other than the original Money Couple, Scott and Bethany Palmer. They wrote about the shocking discovery that 70 percent of divorcing couples cite money troubles as the reason for separation. For Scott and Bethany this was a revelation. I was surprised by the statistic at first, but the more I thought about it, the more sense it made. Our marriage hadn't been without financial drama, and fights about money had us really questioning things in the first few years after we tied the knot.

Since we were able to conquer our money issues and

find renewed strength in our marriage because of it, we were convinced we needed to join the cause and help those struggling couples. If money is at the root of that many broken marriages, and we knew through personal experience that those differences could be managed, then it seemed we had a responsibility to use our expertise to help put a dent in this staggering divorce rate. That's why we committed ourselves to figuring out what it takes for couples to stop fighting about money and start working together to build the life they always dreamed of. Between Scott and Bethany's work and our experience, we think we've cracked the code.

It boils down to this: you and your spouse have a Money Relationship. It's at the core of the way you make decisions about money. Understanding how that Money Relationship works is essential to a thriving, healthy marriage. That's what this book is all about.

The Marital Mix

Recognizing that every couple has a Money Relationship that ripples through their entire marriage was a huge step in our efforts to help ourselves and other couples. We started to really dig into the work we'd done in our own relationship and realized how thorough and complex our Money Relationship was.

At the center of any relationship is two people—two unique individuals with different ideas and feelings and education about money. If you and your spouse felt the same way about sex, you'd never argue about sex. If you felt the same way about how to discipline your children or how often to visit your parents or how important it is to talk about your feelings, you'd never have any conflict. But that's not how people work, because we're all different. Thank God for that—the world would be a boring place if we were all exactly the same.

When it comes to a Money Relationship, couples assume they ought to see things exactly the same way all the time. When they don't, they wonder why their spouse is such an idiot about money. Of course that's the wrong way to look at things. Every person has a unique way of thinking about and dealing with finances—they have their own Money Personality.

As we've worked with couples, we've boiled it down to five Money Personalities. When two people start building a life together, it's only a matter of time before their Money Personalities start to play into the decisions they make. This includes everything from where to eat dinner to what kind of shoes to buy to what kind of wedding to have.

Discovering your Money Personalities (which you'll be doing in chapter 3) will be a revelation in your marriage. It will uncover a part of you that you likely never gave much thought to before. You'll start to understand the very particular way you think about and deal with money, and you'll see that your way might be nothing like the way your spouse thinks about and deals with money. It's going to be one of those "aha!" moments.

You'll have another one of those moments when you and your spouse talk about the ways in which your Money

Personalities both complement and clash with each other. That recurring conversation about how much you spend on shoes? Now you can get to the root of that disagreement. Your spouse's reluctance to buy you something for Valentine's Day? A little analysis will show it's not that he's just being a jerk.

Sometimes the combination of different Money Personalities can create serious tension and conflict, as was the case in our marriage before we developed the vocabulary to talk about what was really happening. Once you understand your partner's Money Personality, the shift in your relationship will blow your mind. If you're willing to stick with us, we're going to help you uncover the connection that led to your marriage in the first place. God created each one of us with very distinct personalities. That beautiful uniqueness is part of our DNA and affects everything we do. It's crucial that we understand that this also includes our approach to money. We believe that this God-given uniqueness is something to be celebrated as well as acknowledged, nurtured, and developed *in tandem* with our spouses.

Make It Happen

We have a saying that you'll find throughout this book, *Make It Happen*. We believe most couples long for a relationship that works; they just need help to break out of old patterns and methods of dealing with money issues. *Make It Happen* is our way of telling you we believe you have what it takes to change the course of your Money

Relationship. We've got the tools to help you, but the motivation must come from you. If you're serious about making a change, if you're willing to commit to taking an honest look at yourself and your relationship, you can overcome any challenge. We've seen countless couples recover from years of conflict, secrecy, even separation, and rebuild a marriage that's worth celebrating. If they can do it, you can too.

To make the most of the tools in this book, we suggest you read it together. You'll be finding out how you deal with money as a person—that's your Money Personality. You'll be discovering potential areas of money conflict in your marriage—we call this the Opposite Dynamic. You'll be gaining invaluable insight on how to turn those conflicts into cooperation—what we refer to as the Fair Fight. All of this will be far more effective if both of you are reading and making these discoveries together.

We also suggest taking it slowly. There is a lot of information in this book, and we want you to really understand each idea before you move on to the next. Don't rush this. The intention is that this book will take you twelve weeks—or about ninety days—to get through, so we recommend reading a chapter or two a week and letting the ideas settle in a bit before you move on. Talk to each other about what you're reading. See what your spouse is thinking as these ideas start to take hold. At the end of each chapter, you'll find a simple exercise to help you integrate the concepts into your marriage. They're quick and easy, but they're essential to putting all the pieces together. They are the way you'll be able to *Make It Happen*.

A final request before you read on past this introduction:

We want to make sure you're in this for real. We want you to make a promise to each other that you are ready to change the way you think about and deal with money as a couple. This is a lifestyle change, not a short-term plan or a one-shot deal. Like a diet or exercise plan, these ideas aren't going to stick unless you decide you are done with the habits that led you to this point. You'll be working on a new way of relating to each other so that you can protect and preserve your relationship.

We'll be asking you to take an honest look at yourselves and to make some significant changes for the sake of your relationship. When it feels like too much, when you're ready to give up, come back to this promise and remind yourselves that there's nowhere to go but forward. Remember, it only takes ninety days to change your marriage for the better.

If you're committed to doing what it takes to discover your Money Personalities and build a healthy Money Relationship, sign below.

_____

By signing my name, I promise my spouse that I will work on our Money Relationship. I will be honest, I will be committed, and I will do my best to understand my spouse and respect the differences in our Money Personalities. Together, we can make change.

Make It Happen!
THE MONEY COUPLE
TAYLOR AND MEGAN KOVAR

IF you're married and want to have a great marriage, it's a choice. No one can make your marriage happy except you. Don't be embarrassed to go to counseling, don't be embarrassed to use resources, read books together, pray together, and learn together.

After all, we're on the same team.

PART 1

≷ WHERE IT ALL BEGINS ≷

ONE

When Love and Money Collide

IT'S right there in our marital vows: for richer or for poorer.

We stand up at our wedding and make these promises, fully expecting that we will stand by each other no matter what. The moment is genuine and pure as we take the first step into a future full of promise.

Every marriage starts with these big hopes and dreams. You walk down the aisle celebrating the ways you connect and complement each other, along with all those little moments of excitement, joy, and intimacy that have been the building blocks of your relationship. For a while those hopes and dreams and joys are enough to carry you into that new life as Mr. and Mrs.

And then life happens. It doesn't matter if things go along just as you planned or if your plans get derailed early on. Life, no matter how great it is, pushes a lot of our biggest hopes and dreams to the side. You start careers. You have kids. You buy a house. You lose a house. Your parents get older. You find yourselves stressed out by the present and worried about the future.

Over time, through no fault of your own, those dreams you had for your married life get put on the back burner, and one by one, they start to dry up and disappear. The dream to buy a house? No longer affordable. The dream to go back to school? No longer feasible with a baby on the way. The dream to backpack through Europe? No longer realistic with the pressures of a job. The dream of an early retirement? No longer fathomable after the market tanked. Goals of all shapes and sizes get shelved and fade away as the years go by.

Ellen and Jack are a perfect example. When they got married, Ellen was working her way toward a partnership at a small law firm. Jack was a graphic designer and had dreams of starting his own design business. Right away they started saving so Jack would have some start-up capital when the time came to set out on his own. They had a five-year plan and a common goal. Then, after just two years of marriage, Ellen was diagnosed with a chronic illness. Her doctor recommended she cut back her hours at work and try to reduce the stressors in her life. While they had good health insurance through Ellen's job, they still had new expenses to deal with that put a dent in their savings. That meant Jack's dream would have to wait a bit longer.

As Ellen's illness became more manageable, the job market became less stable. It no longer seemed like a good idea for Jack to venture out on his own, especially when he knew plenty of designers who would do anything for a regular job like the one he wanted to leave. So they waited a little longer.

You can see how this plays out, right? Pretty soon five years had passed. After having a couple of kids, ten years had gone by and their wages had to cover a bigger family and a higher mortgage for a larger house. When Jack's mother died and his father moved in with him and Ellen and the kids, it put the final nail in the coffin of those early dreams.

Jack and Ellen would be the first to tell you that they have a great life, that they've made choices they feel good about, and that they are blessed beyond measure. That said, they also admit that they miss dreaming about the future together. "When we got married," Ellen said, "I remember talking about how fantastic it would be for Jack to have his own company and really make his mark in the design world. His eyes would light up when we talked about it. Now most of our conversations are like business meetings— who's doing what and when. I know he wouldn't trade our life now for anything, but I'd sure like to see that look in his eyes again."

THERE IS SOMETHING *life-affirming* IN DREAMING TOGETHER AS A COUPLE.

It's a reminder that you are stronger together than you are apart. It's a way of saying to your spouse, "I look forward to the future with you."

If you've lost track of the dreams you used to have, we believe you can get them back. We believe you can reclaim the life you envisioned, one dream at a time.

The Money Part

There's a reason we make a vow to stick together for richer or poorer. Money ripples into every part of our lives as couples; no matter how much of it you have, it can test every aspect of a relationship. If you think about the dreams you had when you got married, almost every one of them had a financial component—buying a house, having children, getting a job, moving to a new city, traveling, spending time with friends . . . the list goes on and on. Money doesn't equal happiness, but it does play a part in whether we can turn our dreams into realities. When finances inevitably come between us and our dreams, we get very unhappy and look for someone or something to blame; and guess who's almost always sitting right there? That's right—our spouses.

Megan and I (Taylor) have met with all types of couples. It doesn't take long to recognize the ones who have lost sight of the dreams they had way back on their wedding day. It doesn't matter if they're rich or poor, if they've been married for forty years or four months or if they know that money is the cause of their problems or are still naive to that fact. These couples sit there and barely talk to or look at each other. When they do speak their words are filled with blame, resentment, and anger. Life hasn't turned out as they'd hoped, and that makes them bitter.

These people come to us because they believe that having a better budget will help. They hope that investing some money in just the right stocks or properties will lead to the retirement they'd always dreamed of. Unfortunately, the budget isn't the problem, and a better portfolio won't solve much either. Even if we offer clear-cut solutions to those problems, without the ability to communicate and work on budgets and investments *together*, it doesn't matter how effective their financial strategy is. The relationship will still sink.

Most couples have no idea how to talk to each other about the money component of a decision. They don't know how to compromise or listen to each other, which makes it impossible for them to come up with a plan that meets both parties' needs. Instead they fight. They blame each other. They resent each other and hurt each other and hide money from each other. Then, feeling like they're out of options, they divorce.

It doesn't have to be that way.

Reviving Your Dreams

Here's the thing: Every decision you make as a couple involves money. Every. Single. One. Money factors into everything, from the type of house you live in to where you go on vacation, from the brand of shampoo you use to the kind of bread you eat. It doesn't matter if we're talking about a $5 cup of coffee or a $50,000 car—money is part of every piece of our lives.

That's why couples who disagree about money will disagree about *everything*.

The combination of love and money is what makes up your Money Relationship. Just like your physical relationship is about much more than sex, and your emotional relationship is about far more than your feelings, your Money Relationship involves a whole lot more than your money. It's about how and why you connect—or don't—when you make decisions where money is involved. It's the deeper set of assumptions and beliefs you bring to those late-night talks about your bank account.

The goal of this book is to help couples stop fighting about money and repair their Money Relationship, regardless of their financial situation. We want to change the way you communicate about money. We want to give you practical, efficient, easy-to-remember, easy-to-apply tools to help you build a stronger Money Relationship. Most important, we want to rekindle your passion for the future—and for each other.

Back when you started dating, you couldn't help but dream together. You were so excited to learn about each other, to discover your sweetheart's favorite food or most embarrassing memory. You wanted nothing more than to know and understand each other. You could talk for hours, dreaming of the life you'd build together. This is the day to start dreaming again. We believe that every couple can recover the love, intimacy, and dreams they had when they first fell in love.

Make It Happen

RECAPTURE that desire to discover new things about your spouse. Take turns telling each other little tidbits the other person might not know, even after years of being together.

TWO

Your Money Relationship

LET'S start by really delving into this idea of the Money Relationship. It's kind of ironic that most of the couples we meet have no concept of their Money Relationship, even though the only reason they want to talk to us is because of money and how it's affecting their relationship. It just doesn't occur to people that the way they deal with money as individuals will influence the way they deal with money as a couple.

Instead, couples tend to think that if they just get a really great financial plan in place, they'll stop arguing about who's buying what. They think that if they can stick with a budget or put enough away for retirement or start building their savings then their money problems will be over. Sadly, that's not the way things work. They can fix the budget, stock up for retirement, even load up the savings account, and still have a lousy Money Relationship. Honestly, what good is a budget if you can't stand each other? What good is that retirement fund or savings account if your relationship is a mess?

What It's Not

Your Money Relationship has nothing to do with your budget. It has nothing to do with your savings. It has nothing to do with how much debt you have or how much you spend every month. That's your financial arrangement—your debt, retirement, taxes, insurance, investing, estate planning, and so on.

Your Money Relationship is about the daily decisions you make as a couple in which money is involved. We even emphasized it to show you how important it is!

NOT WHEN YOU FEEL LIKE IT. IT'S ABOUT **DAILY DECISIONS**.

Before we move on, we want you to really understand the difference between your finances and your Money Relationship. Your financial plans, your debt, your investments, your taxes, your budget—that's one aspect of your life together. As important as those things may be, that's not what this book is about. We want you to focus on the relationship *behind* that part of your life. That's the part that ties your marriage to all those little day-to-day decisions about money.

Here's an example of what we mean: Jonell and Kai have been married for fourteen years. They make a fairly good living; he's an accountant at a hospital, and she does fundraising for a small nonprofit. They have owned their modest house for eight years. They have a bit of student loan debt left to pay off and one car payment. They tend to use credit cards to pay for nearly everything, but they pay off their cards nearly every month. Kai has a 401(k) through work, but they haven't thought all that much about their retirement funds. Their main financial goal right now is to put aside a decent amount of money to help their two children pay for college.

We've given you a pretty good picture of Kai and Jonell's financial situation. You know they have some debt, some savings goals, and some money in a retirement fund. You understand the basics of their financial life. Still, those details tell you nothing about their Money Relationship.

Digging deeper, Kai and Jonell have some real challenges. Kai, the accountant, is obviously good at balancing a budget and figuring out where to save and where to spend. It has naturally fallen on him to handle the financials in their marriage. Jonell, despite being in a finance-oriented field herself, isn't all that interested in how much they bring in each month or how much they pay out. She knows Kai has it taken care of, and she doesn't think twice about it.

Meanwhile Kai worries about their money constantly. Every evening he looks over their credit card account to see how much they spent that day. He lies awake silently calculating where they can cut back to make sure they pay off the bill that month. Those rare months when they have to settle for a minimum or partial payment feel like a failure to him.

If Jonell buys a new outfit for a fundraising event, Kai mentally cancels plans to take her out for a nice dinner then quietly resents his wife for pushing their monthly budget to its limits. He worries that they won't have enough for their retirement, much less enough to help the kids with college. He's considered talking to Jonell about his concerns, but he knows she gets defensive when they talk about money. He does his best to keep his worries to himself.

While their financial picture is perfectly healthy, their Money Relationship is anything but. He's a wreck, she's clueless, and neither of them has any idea that this is a crisis in the making. It won't be long before Kai either explodes at Jonell for her spending or develops an ulcer from worrying about it. Jonell certainly doesn't get a free pass since her willingness to wash her hands of the family finances isn't a sign of trust but rather a sign of disrespect for Kai. Why should he bear the full weight of decisions that have an impact on the whole family?

Most couples have no idea that there is a difference between their finances and their Money Relationship. When they try to solve financial problems that are really the result of these underlying issues, they end up frustrated. Unless couples get to the root of the problem—the challenges in their Money Relationship—they just can't move forward.

We worked with a couple who had been married for more than forty years and who we'd known in the community for quite some time. One afternoon we sat down with them and received the news that they were getting a divorce.

All their financial plans were in place and had been for a long time. But behind those perfect plans were resentment and hurt feelings and misunderstanding. The problem was that they never acknowledged their different perspectives on money; every decision they had made in the past forty years had just added another straw of resentment to the proverbial camel's back. Their plans were solid, but their relationship had fallen apart.

They had plenty of money, and they'd managed it fairly well. The problem? She thought they needed more money in their retirement accounts, and he didn't. She'd been anxious about their future for years and had nagged him about putting more away. Since he felt confident they'd be fine, he had stopped listening to her concerns years before their breaking point. The closer they got to retirement, the more the problem came to a head until she couldn't take it anymore and bailed.

On the surface, their impending divorce was the result of poor financial planning. Looking a little deeper, it wasn't their assets or IRAs that were the problem. It was their total lack of communication. We've never seen a couple break up over their 401(k) performance. We've never seen a couple get divorced because they didn't have enough life insurance or because their estate planning wasn't complete or because they didn't pay off their student loans in less than five years. **What kill relationships are miscommunication and misunderstanding.** That's especially true when it comes to money because, as we've said, it has an impact on every aspect of life.

We often ask couples to tell us about the last money

decision they made. Most of them come up with some investment or a savings plan or a big purchase. It's not until we prompt them to think smaller that they realize every moment of the day ties back to money in one way or another.

Think about it: Do you take a long shower or a money-saving short shower? Coffee at home or a fancy drink whipped up by a barista on your way to work? Generic cereal or the name-brand stuff? Drive to the office or take public transportation? Bag lunch or eat out? Squeeze in some overtime or go back home to the family?

If you and your spouse have fundamental disagreements about money—how much to spend, how much to save, how much risk is too much—then each of those seemingly innocent decisions about hot water, coffee, and lunch are fraught with meaning. Take a long shower when your spouse is trying to cut back on the utility bill, and you've just created a problem. Grab breakfast at the coffee shop when you've agreed to an eat-at-home budget, and you've stirred the hornet's nest.

Because money trickles down to just about every decision

we make during the day, it's not surprising that couples clash about overspending. It's like a constant pop quiz, one you're bound to fail unless you and your spouse have a strong Money Relationship.

Breaking the Cycle

What we see repeatedly is couples who are caught up in a cycle of assumptions, misunderstanding, and blame. It doesn't matter if they have a healthy bank account or are deep in debt, because money isn't actually the problem. Their Money Relationship is the problem.

It took me (Taylor) years to see this, not just in my marriage but also in my work. I'd been working in wealth management for a while before I realized something was a little off. I'd meet with clients, put together airtight financial plans for them, and still hear about problems on the home front and all sorts of stress relating to financial issues. It didn't make sense. I figured if I did my job right, all of the conflicts around money would go away. Unfortunately, that was not the case.

That was the beginning of my realization that there was something deeper than the financial plan. It wasn't the money itself creating these issues; it was that couples had no idea how to talk about money in a way that helped them work together to capitalize on my advice and build the future they'd always dreamed of. I'd been focusing on the "how" behind their financial plans instead of the "why."

I toiled with this until Megan had me think about our

own personal financial journey. She humbly pointed out the role our unique Money Relationship had played in our success. I finally understood that it's not enough to have your financial ducks in a row. You need to know why you think about and deal with money the way you do.

Think about the last time you and your spouse argued about money. For most couples, those arguments are rarely about the actual dollars and cents and instead are rooted in deeper relationship issues like trust, respect, and connection.

Take Mitch and Karen, for example. Mitch loves his coffee. Absolutely loves it. If he can't start his morning with a twenty-ounce double shot from his favorite coffee shop, his whole day is off. Karen, meanwhile, doesn't understand why Mitch would pay almost six bucks a day to feed his habit when she brews a perfectly good pot of coffee at home every morning for pennies. She's tired of watching Mitch spend more than $100 a month on something she sees as totally unnecessary. One morning she lets him know he needs to cut back.

Here's how the conversation goes:

KAREN: You've got to stop hitting the coffee shop every morning. It's too expensive.

MITCH: It is not. Besides, I love their coffee.

KAREN: I make coffee here every morning. Why can't you just drink that?

MITCH: It's not the same. What's the big deal?

KAREN: The big deal is that it costs too much!

MITCH: It's a few bucks, and it makes me happy. What's wrong with that?

KAREN: This isn't about your happiness. It's about you
spending too much money.

MITCH: Why are you so cheap all the time? I just want
to get a cup of coffee!

KAREN: I'm not cheap! I'm trying to keep us from
spending money we don't have!

MITCH: This is ridiculous.

Mitch walks away feeling controlled, and Karen walks away feeling disrespected. They're both hurt and upset, and yet it has nothing to do with the money.

Disagreements like this go to the heart of your relationship. They are the kind of conflicts that linger—every time Mitch heads to the coffee shop, he's going to be irritated at Karen all over again, and she's going to get mad at Mitch all over again. This is the kind of conflict that gets worse over time because couples simply don't know how to fix it. And since every decision you make as a couple has a money component, conflicts like this come up over and over and over again. It's a terrible cycle.

Until you learn to understand your Money Relationship, the cycle will continue.

Bringing Love and Money Together

Your Money Relationship isn't about the plans you make with your money; it's about the reasons you make those plans. You save for a house because you dream of settling down together. You save for college because you dream of a bright future for your children. You plan for retirement because you dream of traveling together one day. You buy lavish gifts for your spouse because you dream of showing them how much they mean to you. You clip coupons and buy day-old bread because you dream of keeping your family financially secure.

You and your spouse started your lives together with those dreams. Now it's time to do what it takes to reclaim your hope, to quit arguing about money, and to heal your Money Relationship.

Neither my wife nor I (Taylor) are therapists (though I do cohost *The Millionaire Marriage* podcast with a marriage and family therapist and have one on staff at my wealth management firm), but we've worked with hundreds of couples as they've tried to repair their fractured unions. Over and over we've seen that when a couple's Money Relationship isn't working, nothing else in the marriage is going well either. It's when couples know how to communicate about money, when they understand each other's approach to finance, and when they build a strong Money Relationship that they grow stronger as a pair.

We want to show you how your love and money come together to help you create a lifestyle that works. We know it's not always easy to turn a relationship around. It takes time to change old habits and replace them with patience and grace and understanding. It takes intentional effort to break out of the cycle of blame and frustration and learn to really listen and rediscover each other. No matter how bleak things seem, we believe you can do this. We've seen so many couples come back from the brink of divorce by making the decision to repair their Money Relationship. Whether you've been married five months or fifty years, we are confident you can be one of those success stories too.

Our hope for you isn't that you come away with more money in your bank account. It's that you come away with a strong, healthy, thriving Money Relationship.

Make It Happen

WHAT are three decisions you made this week? What was the money component? Remember, it's not just the big decisions that involve money, but the little ones too.

THREE

Getting to Know Me: The Five Money Personalities

NO one is neutral about fruitcake. You either love the stuff or hate it. No in-between, no gray area, you're either all in or all out. It's as simple as that.

Money works the same way. There are people who hate to spend money. They feel real, physical pain when they have to pay a bill that's more than expected. Conversely, there are people who love to spend money. They get an adrenaline rush just thinking about their next purchase. There are people who have no qualms about risking everything they have on a big investment and people who would rather stuff all their money into a sock drawer than take a chance on a six-month album. Then there are those people who never think about money. They spend it when they have it and save it if someone reminds them to, but they have no emotional ties to their money. It's a non-issue in their lives.

Just like fruitcake, you don't have to put any thought into this. You know what side of the money debate you fall on.

Megan and I (Taylor) have never questioned our differences. I am much more compelled to spend, and she is much more inclined to save. Back when I didn't have money, my approach got me into a lot of debt. (Remember the 'Stang?) Now I'm in a better place and looking for ways to put the money I have to work. Meanwhile my wife needs that safety net in place at all times. She doesn't want to feel like the way I use money is putting our family's security at risk.

At first I didn't understand why my spending might bother her. Especially when I could point to my revenue and prove that I hadn't spent more than I made. It took a lot of conversing and dissecting our Money Personalities before we came to a very simple realization: people have intrinsically different ways of thinking about money.

Somewhere in the back of my mind, I always assumed we'd get on the same page once we shared a bank account and were on firm financial ground. In hindsight, that was very naive thinking. We have different backgrounds, experiences, and relationships with money. Those traits and habits are ingrained in us and are not going to change anytime soon (or ever).

Coming to terms with this truth—that my wife and I would never have the same financial DNA—made it that much easier to understand where other friends, family, and clients were coming from.

I thought about our friend's mom who is the queen of saving money. She goes with generic brands, buys bread at the discount bakery, and does it all with a smile. Buying the less expensive item is a victory for her, not some sort of admission of defeat. It has nothing to do with how much she has in the bank; it's just that she loves saving money. Finding deals is her favorite pastime, and it's not a bad one to have.

On the flip side is our friend Carla. She doesn't think about money, doesn't worry about what she's spent or how much she's made. The balance of her bank account is all but an irrelevant detail. She works freelance and occasionally forgets to invoice clients. Even with all that uncertainty that would drive someone like our friend's mom or my wife utterly insane, Carla's happy. She tries to find good deals and doesn't live beyond her means, but otherwise gives the whole money thing very little thought.

Both the queen-of-saving mom and happy-go-lucky Carla deal with money in ways that are vastly different from how either Megan or I deal with it. No one way is superior to another, as much as we want to think our approach is the best. If you tend toward saving, anyone who spends carelessly is making a bad choice. If you love to buy stuff, the more frugal crowd lives too rigidly and doesn't know how to enjoy life.

We all know people with vastly different spending habits than our own. Everyone has that cheap friend who never seems to pay for anything, or the coworker who throws in $5 on a group gift when everyone else put in $20, or the coupon queen who never met a deal she didn't like. We also know people who seem to spend indiscriminately—the shopaholic who can't resist one more purchase, or the big-spending buddy who always buys another round.

We know people who will always take a financial bet—investing in the latest multi-level marketing business or buying shares of some company they know about in Sri Lanka. We know people who've planned for every possible problem the future might hold—flood insurance and fire insurance and dismemberment insurance and pet insurance and kidnapping insurance and on and on. And we also know people like Carla, who don't think about money at all.

The bottom line is that everyone thinks about and deals with money in a unique, highly personal way. That's because each of us has something we call a *Money Personality*. There are five of them:

1. Security Seeker
2. Saver
3. Spender
4. Risk Taker
5. Flyer

Each of the five Money Personalities has its strengths and its challenges. Each of them can help you make great financial decisions, and each of them has the potential to get you into financial trouble. That's why we remind people that there is no right or wrong Money Personality. They are what they are. The goal of discovering your Money Personality isn't to point out your flaws but, rather, to help you understand yourself and the way you spend (or don't spend) your paychecks. The more you know about yourself and your financial perspectives, the better equipped you are to work with your spouse to build a strong Money Relationship.

Finding Your Money Personality

Before we dig any deeper into the Money Personalities, we want you to read through the descriptions and figure out which of them seems to fit you the best. You're actually going to choose two of the five—a Primary Money Personality and a Secondary Money Personality. As you read through the descriptions, you'll find one that strikes you as absolutely true to who you are when it comes to money. That's your Primary Money Personality. There will be a second one that hits close to home as well but isn't quite as strong. That's your Secondary Money Personality.

For example, Taylor's Primary Money Personality is Spender. He can spend money with the best of them, sometimes to my dismay. His Secondary Money Personality is Risk Taker. When there's an investment to be made, chances are he's going to make it. As you might expect, this combination has pros and cons. When the risk is worth taking, I (Megan) love that Taylor's willing to take it. When the risk isn't worth the reward, I have to give Taylor one of my loving but stern talks about reeling it in.

For a long time we thought people just had one Money Personality, but the more we looked at ourselves and our Money Personalities, the more we realized that the individual personalities weren't mutually exclusive. You can be a Saver and a Risk Taker, a Spender and a Flyer, a Security Seeker and a Saver. Not only is it possible to have more than one—it's highly likely.

We'll talk more about how your Primary and Secondary Money Personalities work together in the next chapter. For now all we want you to do is identify the Money Personalities that fit you best. We'll get into the nitty-gritty soon enough.

Your Primary Money Personality will be easy to figure out. You'll instantly recognize yourself in the descriptions to follow. Your Secondary Money Personality is less obvious, but it often shows up when you're feeling stressed about your finances. For example, if you're a Saver who worries you won't have enough money in the bank to cover an emergency, you're probably a Saver/Security Seeker. If you're a Saver who skimps on the little things so you can afford to splurge now and then, you're probably a Saver/Risk Taker.

If you aren't sure or you just want more details about each type, you can find a free Money Personality quiz on our website, TheMoneyCouple.com. With the help of statistical scientist Dr. Kirk Cameron, we've developed this tool to confirm exactly what your Money Personalities are. It's a simple quiz that takes less than ten minutes to complete, and the results will have a profound impact on you and your relationship.

Ours looks like this:

	taylor	megan
1 PRIMARY	**SPENDER**	**SAVER**
2 SECONDARY	**RISK TAKER**	**SECURITY SEEKER**

You can use this one or make your own!

1 PRIMARY		
2 SECONDARY		

Once you've figured out your Primary and Secondary Money Personalities, ask your spouse to do the same. You'll both need this information as you work through the remaining chapters of the book.

The Money Personalities

Saver

Ed is a Saver. How do we know? Well, Ed is the kind of guy who washes his Ziploc bags. He reuses aluminum foil. If he finds a piece of rotting fence in an alley, he brings it home and tucks it away in his workroom in case he finds a use for it later. He has little plastic bins full of old faucets and knobs, jars of rusty screws and bent nails, three hammers that he got at a garage sale for a dime apiece, and at least three old lawnmowers he is pretty sure he can fix.

If Ed sounds a lot like your grandpa, that's because he is. Except that Ed is a thirty-eight-year-old high school physics teacher.

Like most Savers, Ed never met a deal he didn't like. However, as far as Ed is concerned, free beats cheap every time, even if the thing he's getting is old, broken, or even useless. He'd rather recycle that old rotten fence into some sort of woodworking project than buy new stuff at the lumberyard at half price.

Ed's junk collection is just the tip of his Saver iceberg. He drives a car with no air conditioning, his driver's side door doesn't close all the way in the winter, and his vehicle is missing its ignition panel—he has to start it with a screwdriver. Most of his wardrobe is made up of clothes he's had since college and shirts his wife buys him for Christmas. His favorite shoes are a pair of high-end loafers he got at the thrift store for $7—a bit more than he felt comfortable spending, but his wife convinced him they were a very good deal.

Ed is, obviously, a fairly extreme example of a Saver. Not every Saver is a pack rat. Not every Saver objects to buying something new. Megan is a Saver, and she owns twice the amount of clothing I do and always looks more fashionable. I (Taylor) work with some Savers worth millions, and they got that way by watching every penny. We know Savers who drive nice cars and live in nice houses and go on nice vacations, and they pay for all of it up front, in cash.

While Savers don't always save in the same ways, there are some traits that are common to most of them. You're a Saver if you:

Get a genuine rush from saving money. It's a source of pride to get something you wanted for less.

Are organized, responsible, and trustworthy when it comes to finances. A Saver won't tap out the kids' college fund to pay for a new boat. A Saver won't toss a twenty into the office basketball pool.

Rarely spend impulsively. Savers will scour the internet for deals, plan every detail of a vacation, and make sure they have the money in hand before making a purchase.

Avoid credit card debt like head lice. Savers hate paying interest and accruing debt. They want to pay off every bill, in full, right away.

As we mentioned, every Money Personality has its challenges. If you're a Saver, you need to be aware that you can be:

A joy stealer. If you're a Saver and your partner isn't, your resistance to spending money can suck the fun out of everything from seeing a movie to going on vacation. I have been known to get a little frustrated from time to time when Megan pulls the reins on my spending.

Overly focused on financial goals. A main cause of Savers being joy stealers is that they tend to think too intently about money. It's great to have firm financial goals and to work hard to meet them, but sometimes Savers need to swallow their anxiety and let themselves, and others, just enjoy life.

Cheap. Savers have a hard time parting with their money, so much so that they may come across as cheap and even selfish to others.

Savers can be great partners because they are careful about spending and usually make wise financial choices. Speaking from experience, being married to a Saver has changed my life for the better and has allowed me to do things like write this book with her. The challenge for Savers is to see money as a means to an end, not an end in itself.

Spender

Colleen is a Spender. If there's a chance to spend money, she'll spend it. Friends coming over for dinner? That's the perfect excuse for a bundle of fresh flowers and some cute new dessert plates. A Saturday spent running errands? Might as well grab lunch with a friend to break up the day. By May she's already got a closet full of Christmas gifts. Those displays right by the checkout counter at every store? Colleen can't resist them—she'll grab a pack of gum, a little toy for her daughter, a couple of tubes of lip balm—whatever looks interesting or new or necessary.

For Colleen spending isn't about having more stuff. She's far more likely to buy a gift for a friend than to spend money on herself. She's the first to pick up the tab when she has coffee with a coworker, always shows up at a party with something to share with everyone, and has a reputation for giving generously when there's a need in her church community or her children's school.

Colleen's spending has gotten her into some financial pickles. She has bounced a few checks in her time, and she amassed a fair bit of debt before she was married and handed the finances over to her husband. Fortunately, she's learned that she doesn't have to spend a lot of money to get the rush of joy that comes from shopping and giving. Those little items from the checkout line make her just as happy as the cart full of expensive swag.

Spenders don't care how much they spend or who they spend it on. They aren't necessarily rich; we know plenty of Spenders who can do some serious shopping at the dollar store. Spenders just like spending. You're a Spender if you:

Live in the moment. Spenders are focused on what's happening right now, and they are willing to spend whatever is in their wallets to make life a blast. They might have less money down the road, but for the Spender, it's all about making memories today.

Love to buy things for other people. Spenders get a lot of joy out of giving gifts, helping out, and treating other people.

Get a thrill from the purchase. It doesn't matter if you're shopping at Saks or at the Salvation Army thrift store. The price doesn't matter nearly as much as the fun of buying.

If you're a Spender, and I say this with a great deal of self-awareness, you should know that you can be:

Impractical. Spenders are often impulse buyers. A Spender walks into a store without lists and without limits. Spenders don't do research to find a good deal; we do research to find the thing we want most. This problem is exacerbated by the fact that we don't do well differentiating between wants and needs.

Noncommunicative. All that impractical impulse buying means that Spenders don't think—much less talk—through purchases with their partners. This lack of communication can come across as secretive and sneaky to the Spender's spouse.

Filled with regret. As a card-carrying Spender, Christmas is just the best for me (Taylor). Megan always tries to get me to dial it back, but I can't resist buying too many presents for everyone in the family. Come January, I'm able to step back and see that, once again, she was right and I overdid it.

A budget breaker. Spenders can put together a mean budget. They can also have great intentions when it comes to sticking to said budget. Then, unsurprisingly, that doesn't happen. That leads them—and their unwilling spouses—into serious, life-altering debt. Spenders might even feel bad about the overspending, but they have a hard time stopping themselves. This can be unbearably frustrating for the Spender's spouse.

A Spender can be a great partner, rarely letting finances get in the way of enjoying life. The big challenge for us is to respect the money expectations of our loved ones, particularly when your wife is a Saver (and currently reading over my shoulder as I write this section. Kidding!)

Risk Taker

You've probably met someone like Patrice. She's that person who is always up to something interesting. When she goes on vacation, it's never somewhere like Florida or the Grand Canyon. No, Patrice heads to a beach in Vietnam or goes ice climbing in Canada. When she goes out to eat, it's to that new place that opened in a warehouse downtown or a little hole-in-the-wall joint you've never heard of. She's the first to try out a new tech gadget, the first to tell you about some band she discovered at a music festival in Tucson, the first to bike to work in the snow.

Patrice is a Risk Taker, not just in her travel plans and restaurant choices but in her finances as well. She's not afraid to invest in a friend's business venture or chip in to help a buddy make his independent film. She has a good job and a healthy disposable income, and she sees no reason to let her money sit in a bank account when she can use it to be part of something amazing, intriguing, or innovative.

She has taken a hit more than once. She and a friend of a friend went in on a food cart business that never really took off, and now she's the proud owner of an industrial-grade chest freezer. She bought a run-down house with the intention of flipping it, but the housing market tanked, and she's stuck with a property she can't sell. Despite these financial setbacks, Patrice is always looking for the next big thing, the next opportunity to plunge headfirst into an adventure. One of these days she knows it's going to play out perfectly.

For Risk Takers, the thrill of jumping into a financial challenge doesn't just come from a huge payout on an investment; it comes from taking the risk in the first place. Even if they never hit it big, Risk Takers continue to chase that rush they get from trying out a new idea. It's just how they're wired. If you're a Risk Taker, you:

Are a big-picture person. Risk Takers aren't always worried about details. They don't get hung up on the *how* of an idea. Instead, they get a lead on something—a business opportunity, an investment option, a real estate deal—and they move. Fast.

Love finding the next adventure. For Risk Takers, no idea is too out there, no risk too big. Their sense of adventure takes over, and they want in.

Get excited by possibility. Risk Takers get more excited about the idea of something than about the thing itself. By the time the deal plays out and they've gotten their return, they've moved on to the next opportunity.

Listen to your gut. More than conventional wisdom or financial experts, intuition is what Risk Takers trust. If a deal doesn't feel right, they won't do it. But if something strikes their fancy, they're on it.

Aren't afraid to make decisions. Risk Takers don't mess around when it comes to money. They make a decision and make it fast. That can be a real plus when there are important decisions on the line.

If you're a Risk Taker, be aware that you can come across as:

Blinded by possibility. When a Risk Taker gets hold of an idea, reason has left the building. Also absent may be concern for other people's feelings, attention to details, and long-term planning.

Easily resented. Even if a Risk Taker is in a relationship with another Risk Taker, the quick decisions and the leveraging of assets can end with two people who don't like each other very much. When a decision pays off, everyone's happy; all it takes is one bum deal to create a rift of resentment.

Impatient. Risk Takers can lose patience with people who don't sign on to their big ideas as quickly as they'd like. Risk Takers often make decisions without consulting the people those decisions affect most—their spouses.

Insensitive. Risk Takers hate feeling hemmed in by other people, so rather than work for compromise, they charge ahead and deal with the relational fallout later. When a Risk Taker's spouse isn't on board with the decision, there's always relational fallout.

This is my (Taylor's) Secondary Personality, a nice complement to my Spender tendencies. Us Risk Takers can deliver great wealth and success to our families as we look ahead with excitement and optimism. Our big challenge is to keep the people we love involved in the decision-making and to recognize when it's time to let an opportunity pass for the sake of the marriage.

Security Seeker

If there were ever a classic Security Seeker, it's Jerry. He eats breakfast at the same restaurant every Saturday. On Casual Fridays at work, he wears his normal work shirt and khaki pants. His favorite vacation spot is the condo he owns two hours from his primary residence.

This predictability doesn't make Jerry boring. He's always up for an adventure, as long as he can plan for it. When a group of college buddies decided to ring in their fortieth birthdays together by renting a sailboat and spending five days on the ocean, Jerry was right there with them. When his anniversary rolls around every year, his wife knows he'll come up with something over-the-top romantic like a weekend getaway or a custom piece of jewelry covered in diamonds.

Like many Security Seekers, Jerry has no problem spending money; he just wants to make sure he's spending wisely. That vacation property? He didn't bite until the price came down and he and his family had already agreed they loved the area. The sailing trip? Jerry mapped out their course, researched rental companies to find one with a solid reputation, and made sure his life insurance was up-to-date. The gifts for his wife? He makes sure their yearly budget includes room for his annual splurge by cutting back on extras for a few weeks.

Jerry's definitely willing to spend money; he's just not willing to do so without verifying his family's security first.

Security Seekers like to know the future is settled and safe. They are all about planning, consistency, and clear expectations. When it comes to money, the Security Seeker's motto is "Better safe than sorry." You're a Security Seeker if you are:

An investigator. Security Seekers would never invest in a piece of property they hadn't seen. In fact, Security Seekers wouldn't just need to see the property; they'd need to have the soil tested for toxicity, look into all the zoning restrictions within a three-mile radius, and get a detailed prospectus from the developer and a resume from every other investor.

Trustworthy. Security Seekers rarely put their futures on the line. That means they aren't likely to spend this month's mortgage on a car or tap into the college fund to join a multi-level marketing company.

Willing to sacrifice. A Security Seeker would rather do without today than do without tomorrow. Security Seekers won't spend money until they know they've got enough to pay the bills, contribute to their retirement, and cover any other obligations they've set up to make sure the foreseeable future is all squared away.

Prepared for anything. Security Seekers are never caught without a plan. The Security Seeker rarely ends up in a crisis (at least not a real crisis—ordinary economic hiccups feel catastrophic to Security Seekers), which means the rest of the family can rest a little easier.

If you're a Security Seeker, you have a tendency to:

Be overly negative. Security Seekers get nervous about risk, so they often say no to every idea that comes along. Security Seekers can become controlling, using their veto power to keep their spouse from taking even the slightest risk or chasing a small dream.

Get stuck in a research rut. We call this tendency "paralysis by analysis." In other words, Security Seekers can get so caught up in avoiding buyer's remorse or making sure an opportunity is foolproof that they never act.

Stifle creativity. This challenge doesn't just affect the other people in the Security Seeker's life; it affects the Security Seeker too. Over time, that need for comfort and predictability can become so all-consuming that they stop looking at the possibilities and stick with the certainties—and that can be a very subtle but impactful form of control.

Security Seeker is my (Megan's) Secondary Personality, and Taylor finds it to be a real blessing as well as a curse. It brings the perfect balance to his personalities, despite putting us at odds from time to time. I'm keen on careful planning and a steady approach to money that helps temper some of my husband's whimsical ideas. The challenge for me and other Security Seekers is to resist making decisions out of fear and to know how much financial security is enough. I usually tell Taylor I'm just being a realist, but I'll admit, sometimes I go a little too far.

Flyer

Finally, we get to the mysterious Flyer. We'll use Brett as our example. He's a musician—he plays in a couple of bands, teaches music, and works in a recording studio as a sound engineer. He lives a fairly unconventional life, and he wouldn't have it any other way.

Brett has lived in at least ten different apartments in five different cities since graduating from college fifteen years ago. He tends to go where the work is and makes a life for himself when he gets there. For the last three years, he and his wife have rented a great old house, but he's starting to get antsy. One of his coworkers told Brett about a studio his friend owns in another state, and Brett and his wife are seriously considering making a move.

Brett's students would be sorry to see him go. He's a gracious, passionate teacher, and he is truly invested in the success of the kids he works with. Their parents love him too. He is easygoing, encourages the kids to work hard, and isn't picky about when they pay him or even how much they pay him for lessons. One of the parents has offered to help Brett set up a more reliable billing system, but Brett thinks that's more work than it's worth. He always gets paid eventually, and he really doesn't have a head for business. He'd just as soon avoid the headache of billing and keeping accounts.

The Flyer is perhaps the most unusual Money Personality. Flyers don't think about the money component of a decision at all. They're not anxious about it; they're not consumed by it; they have absolutely no emotional response to money and tend to fly by the seat of their pants. You're a Flyer if you are:

Basically content with your life. Flyers might be dirt-poor and living in an Airstream out by the highway, but they don't care. As long as Flyers are making their own choices, everything is cool.

Big on relationships. For Flyers, relationships and connections with other people are crucial.

Happy to let someone else take care of your finances. This can be a big plus in relationships, especially if the other partner has one of the other Money Personalities.

Not motivated by money. Most Flyers end up living exactly the lives they want to live because they make choices based on personal fulfillment, not what will make them the most money.

If you're a Flyer, you need to be aware that you can be:

Reactionary. Flyers don't think about money, but money
is a necessary part of life. Sooner or later, even the
flightiest Flyers have to pay attention to their bills
or their looming retirement. When that moment
comes, they often make decisions based on fear
instead of good, sound advice.

Lacking in the skills needed to solve your money problems.
When financial issues come up, Flyers try to handle
it. After a life of not caring about money, they don't
have any idea how money problems are resolved.
Interest? Consolidation? Refinancing? Comparison
shopping? These concepts just aren't on their radar.

Disorganized. Flyers aren't always disorganized people
in the general sense, but when it comes to money,
they are all over the place. We've asked Flyers to
bring in tax returns, and they have no idea where
something like that might be. Some of them don't
even remember if they filed taxes or what their
taxable income is.

Unresponsible. Anyone who isn't a Flyer might think
this should read *ir*responsible, but the Flyer is
actually *un*responsible. Irresponsibility suggests a
deliberate lack of maturity. Flyers aren't trying to
be lazy or inattentive. They genuinely don't think
about money issues.

Flyers can make great spouses because they are impres-
sively easygoing when it comes to finances. The chances

of them being controlling or uptight about money are slim to none. The challenge for Flyers is to stay involved and invested in the family's finances so they contribute instead of detract.

And now you know the five Money Personalities. Having read each description, where do you find yourself? As you go through the rest of the book, we'll keep coming back to your Money Personality, so make sure you have a sense of who you are.

Once you've pegged your Primary Money Personality, don't forget to identify your Secondary Money Personality as well. The interplay of these two has a big impact on your Money Relationship, which you got a glimpse of in the back-and-forth between us Kovars.

IF YOU HAVEN'T ALREADY TAKEN OR WANT TO SHARE THE 5 MONEY PERSONALITIES ASSESSMENT, **SCAN HERE!**

One more note: Now that you have identified your Primary and Secondary Money Personalities, you've probably already figured out which of them fit your spouse too. No matter how sure you are about this, it's essential that you let your spouse determine their own Money Personalities. Part of the process of healing your Money Relationship is for both of you to know yourselves well and understand why you think about money the way you do. If you just assign your spouse a Money Personality without letting them work through the options and do a little self-assessing, the rest of the ideas in this book won't be as effective.

It's easy to read these descriptions and think about all the issues that can come up when couples have different Money Personalities, and we'll touch on that soon enough. For now we want to keep the focus on you as individuals and make sure you truly understand your own Money Personalities and how they affect you.

Your Lens for Life

Your Primary Money Personality is the lens through which you view all your money decisions. It's what motivates you to wait until that sweater is on sale. It's what drives you to put 30 percent of your paycheck in your savings account. It's what makes you buy a round of drinks for your friends. Because money touches every decision you make, your Primary Money Personality frames your entire perspective on life.

We find that people who are Spenders tend to be fairly gregarious. They are generous not only with their money but with their time and talents as well. Spenders love to lavish affection and attention on the people they care about. They are the kind of people who insist you stay with them when you're visiting instead of going to a hotel. They are the ones who offer to drive when you go on double dates or let you choose the restaurant and still insist on paying. They are just bighearted people. They aren't necessarily outgoing, but they are always ready to help out and do what they can for the good of other people.

Savers tend to be more intentional about their money and the other parts of their lives. They rarely make a decision without a lot of forethought. They like plans and clear expectations about relationships, work, even their free time. Savers have a good sense of how much time or effort a project will take and will dole out their energy accordingly. That's why Savers often cultivate a tight circle of friends—in their own way, they conserve their relational funds as deftly as they conserve their money.

The Security Seeker and the Risk Taker personalities create unique lenses for life as well. Security Seekers are unlikely to take risks, personally or professionally. When they plan a vacation, they want to see all the maps, read all the brochures, make all the reservations. Risk Takers are happy to get online and see if there are cheap tickets for the next day to anywhere in the world, knowing they can be packed and ready to go by morning. A Security Seeker loves to settle in for a cozy movie night at home while a Risk Taker will head to the movie theater and pick a flick on-site.

And Flyers? They're content to just go with the flow. They have ideas and opinions, to be sure, but they tend to be easygoing and spontaneous. At work they are often highly creative and easily adaptable. They don't stress out over deadlines, and they aren't easily frazzled. In relationships they let their true feelings show and don't get too worked up over disagreements or conflict. They like to keep things simple and clear.

Naturally, these are broad generalizations, but you get the idea. Of course, there are spontaneous Savers and selfish Spenders, confident Security Seekers and nervous Risk Takers. It's important to recognize that your Money Personalities aren't a separate piece of you; they're fully integrated into other parts of your personality and vice versa. The deeper your recognition of the ways your Money Personalities influence your life and your decisions, the more prepared you are to dig into your Money Relationship and make it stronger.

Take Britt and Alex, for example. They love to travel, and yet almost every time they go on vacation, they end up in a huge argument that ruins the whole trip. They hate it, their kids hate it, and until last year, they had no idea how to fix it. Then they figured out what their Money Personalities were, and they finally started to break the cycle of conflict that was damaging their relationship.

It turns out that Britt is a Saver and Alex is a Risk Taker. They realized that many of their vacation arguments started when Alex went shopping for souvenirs. They loved bringing home reminders of their travels, but they had very different ideas about what those reminders should be. Alex loves to collect art and pottery made by local artists. Britt is happy with a refrigerator magnet and a postcard.

After they discovered their Money Personalities, Britt and Alex had a better sense of why they both felt so strongly about a seemingly trivial issue. For Alex, buying a painting or a ceramic jar from a local artisan was a thrill—who knows how much that original piece could be worth one day? He loved the idea of investing in an unknown artist and being a small part of that person's success. For Britt, her concerns about the money Alex spent far outweighed any appeal the purchase had. She saved and planned their vacation budgets very carefully and had every meal and excursion accounted for. In one afternoon of shopping, Alex could ruin months of hard work.

Instead of leaning into those emotions and having a fight in the gift shop, Britt chose to wait and talk to Alex about her anxiety. She proposed they set a limit on the cost of any souvenirs, and Alex agreed. Going forward, Britt would factor that money into their travel budget, and they had their first fight-free vacation in years.

That's what happens when you know your Primary and Secondary Money Personalities. You can figure out why you become frustrated or angry or controlling or anxious and then do something about it. You suddenly know why it drives you crazy when your spouse goes into the store for a gallon of milk and comes out with milk . . . and doughnuts and a magazine and some batteries and three bags of chips. You finally understand why you feel controlled when your spouse gets mad at you for buying doughnuts and a magazine and some batteries and three bags of chips.

Your Money Personality DNA

When we talk with people about their Money Personalities, they always ask us where these instinctual feelings about money come from. Are you born with them? Are they a response to how you were raised? The answer is yes—*sort of.*

We've come to believe that your Money Personalities are part of your DNA. Though the Money Personality gene hasn't been identified yet, the way you think about money seems to be just something you're born with. When we look at our children, it's obvious that Kix is a Saver/Spender and Kambry is a Spender/Risk Taker (just like her daddy, much to her mommy's dismay).

Even though he's a Saver, our son Kix is going to spend his cash. He doesn't bury money in the backyard or have his grade-school sights set on college. However, the money he gets for allowances, birthdays, and holidays goes toward big-ticket items instead of the first candy bar or cheap toy he can find. He saves for a while and compares the video game prices at Target, Best Buy, and Amazon, then sees how much he can get out of his cash reserves.

And then there's Kambry. When she holds a dollar bill, it's like her fingertips are burning. Instead of planning ahead and saving for a couple months, her dream day is blowing twenty bucks at the Dollar Tree. If I (Megan) gave her $10 to spend at an arcade, she'd manage to spend $20 before I knew what happened. She'd also head straight for the game that took the most tokens, because that little girl never met a financial risk she didn't want to take.

Two kids. Same household. Two very different approaches.

The family you grew up in can have a big influence on how you feel about money, but we find that most people can look back and see signs of their Money Personalities in their childhoods well before they would be intentionally responding to their parents' influence. Phyllis, Taylor's mom, is a serious Security Seeker with Spender as her secondary personality. So while the spending existed in his childhood, the dominant trait was embracing security. Nevertheless, young Taylor was always ready to spend his allowance on the first thing that caught his eye.

Your Money Personalities are as much a part of you as your feelings about fruitcake, and it's just as unlikely to change. Don't fight it. Embrace your Money Personalities and start paying attention to all the ways it plays out in your life. The more you know about how you view money, the better equipped you are to overcome your challenges and start using your strengths to build a better Money Relationship.

Make It Happen

THINK about a time when your Primary
Money Personality has driven a money
decision. Do the same for your Secondary
Money Personality. How have those Money
Personalities been an asset in your life?

FOUR

The Opposite Dynamic

YOUR Money Personalities frame the way you think about money and life. Once you know your Primary and Secondary Personalities, you'll start noticing them playing out in all kinds of ways. If you're a Risk Taker, for example, you'll start to notice the little decisions you make every day that have an element of the unknown to them—checking out a new restaurant, pursuing a new business contact, trying a new recipe. If you're a Saver, you'll notice that you compare prices at the grocery store or automatically head to the outlets if you need new clothes.

Keep in mind that's just your Primary Money Personality at work. Your Secondary Personality, while not as prominent, still has an impact on the way you view money. That's why there are Spenders who experience serious buyer's remorse and Flyers who retire as millionaires.

We've learned that there are certain combinations of Primary and Secondary Money Personalities that create something we call the *Opposite Dynamic*. The Opposite Dynamic is the internal conflict so many of us experience when our Primary and Secondary Money Personalities clash.

Our friend Matt's Primary Money Personality is Spender. His Secondary Personality is Security Seeker. His Spender side loves to shop, as you would expect. A few months ago when he needed a new speaker for his home theater setup, he spent his Saturday morning at the store, did a little looking to find the perfect product, then left with a new speaker. He also loaded a new flat-screen into his car. And a new PlayStation.

For the first five minutes of his drive home, Matt was on the new-stuff high that Spenders get from spending. But then, just a few blocks from his driveway, his Security Seeker side kicked in. What had he just done? What if he needed that money next week? What if the car needed repairs? What if he lost his job? By the time he parked in front of his house, he'd already done the math on what he could return and vowed never to spend so much again.

This response is the result of the Opposite Dynamic. His Primary and Secondary Money Personalities led him to want two very different things: the thrill of the purchase and the security of knowing he has planned for the future.

The Opposite Dynamic is the result of your Money Personalities having competing needs. That competition creates internal tension, and that tension can quickly creep into your Money Relationship. We're going to take some time to break down this idea of the Opposite Dynamic so you can see how that internal tension might be seeping into your marriage.

Clashing Personalities

The five Money Personalities can be put into two groups. On one side are the Spender, the Risk Taker, and the Flyer. These three Money Personalities have a few things in common:

- They think of money as a means to an end.
- They tend to be more impulsive.
- They don't experience much fear or anxiety when it comes to money.

On the other side are the Saver and the Security Seeker. They also have a few things in common:

- They think of money as an end in itself.
- They tend to be intentional spenders.
- They struggle with fear and anxiety when it comes to money.

If your Primary Money Personality is in one group and your Secondary Money Personality is in the other, you have the Opposite Dynamic. There are plenty of benefits to having dueling personalities, but it's much easier to notice the challenges it creates.

Our friend Claire's Primary Money Personality is the Saver, and her Secondary is the Flyer. She got a new job recently, one that called for a more professional wardrobe. That meant Claire needed to go shopping, an activity she very much despises. She put it off until the weekend before her first day at the new job. Instead of having time to look for a good deal or wait for a sale, Claire ended up paying full price for clothes she didn't really like all that much. As a result, instead of feeling confident in her new outfit on that first day of work, all Claire could think about was how much she'd spent.

Claire's Saver side created anxiety about how much she'd paid for the clothes, while her Flyer Money Personality kept her from making plans that could have helped her spend less in the first place. Quintessential Opposite Dynamic.

Like Matt from our earlier example, Claire is dealing with that internal tension between her Primary and Secondary Money Personalities. While it's often easier for people to pay attention to the conflict they feel because of the Opposite Dynamic, we find that the Opposite Dynamic can also be a helpful diagnostic check. If you pay attention to it, it can save you from the challenging parts of your Money Personalities.

Every one of the five Money Personalities has a downside. Spenders can go off the deep end and leave themselves and their families drowning in debt. Savers can be so aggressive in their efforts to save money that they can rob themselves and everyone around them of the joy that comes from living life to the fullest. Risk Takers can be reckless, while Security Seekers can be so fixated on the future that they never enjoy the present. Flyers can find themselves working for thirty years and having made essentially zero financial gains.

Your Secondary Money Personality works as a kind of stopgap that keeps your Primary Personality from running amok, and vice versa. Take Matt, our Spender/Security Seeker. Matt's Secondary Money Personality keeps him focused on the future. When he spends more than he planned to on new devices, his Security Seeker side kicks in and helps him get back on track so that when the car breaks down—because it will—he'll be ready to get it fixed.

At the same time, Matt's Spender Money Personality helps him keep an eye on the here and now. Matt's not so worried about tomorrow that he forgets to enjoy today, even when that means spending some money to make that enjoyment happen. His Opposite Dynamic works to his advantage.

If we look at Claire, we see that her Opposite Dynamic can be an asset as well. She's a Saver, something that can be a lifesaver for a Flyer. Flyers aren't necessarily careless with money, but they don't think about it much. If a Flyer is also a Spender, they can end up dealing with unpaid bills, endless debt, and foreclosure. For Claire, her Saver Personality helps keep her from spending money she doesn't have.

On the flipside, Claire's Flyer Money Personality keeps her Saver side from falling into a spiral of shame and anxiety when she does spend more than she planned. Claire worried about her new job shopping spree for a morning and then moved on. Other things are far more important to Claire than her money.

If you have the Opposite Dynamic between your Primary and Secondary Money Personalities, it might take a little thinking to see how your conflicting approaches can actually help create balance in your life. Once you start to see how the two work together, you'll be moving toward a better understanding of the role you play in building a strong Money Relationship with your spouse.

In the next two chapters, we're going to move from talking about each of you as individuals to dealing with the way your Money Personalities combine as a couple. That's why it's so important to know yourself well before moving on. We want you to identify and own both the good and the not-so-good aspects of your Money Personality, as well as understand how the Opposite Dynamic plays out in the decisions you make about money.

Make It Happen

THINK of three times your Primary and
Secondary Money Personalities have
worked together in a positive way. If you
have the Opposite Dynamic, think about
ways your Primary and Secondary Money
Personalities balance each other out.

FIVE

The Big Reveal: The Five Money Personalities Together

EVERY couple we know argues about money—including us. Money has an impact on every choice and decision, so it only makes sense that some of those decisions will lead to fights about money. For a lot of couples, those fights get personal. "You spend too much!" "You're cheap!" "You're too controlling!" "I can't trust you with our credit cards!" Is there any wonder why money conflicts are behind more than 70 percent of divorces in this country?

There's also something deeply personal about money fights. When we first started helping couples with their Money Relationships, we knew everyone had a Money Personality. We knew that couples argue about money, but what surprised us was how hurtful those arguments could be. In the years since we started this type of financial counseling, we've come to see that there is something about a person's

Money Personality that runs into the core of who that person is. Your Money Personality is part of the lens through which you view your life. So when someone criticizes that view, it feels deeply personal.

That's why we're going to spend the next couple of chapters helping you and your spouse discover each other's Money Personalities. We believe that when you truly understand each other and your perspectives, you'll stop criticizing and instead start working together to build a healthy Money Relationship.

Find out your Money Personalities now at 5MoneyPersonalities.com.

UNDERSTAND YOU AND YOUR
SPOUSE'S MONEY PERSONALITIES.

Before we move on, we want to make sure you and your spouse have identified your Primary and Secondary Money Personalities. Obviously, it's best if both of you are reading this book, but if you're reading it on your own, you can still get your spouse involved.

As noted earlier, here's what *not* to do: *do not* guess your spouse's Money Personality. Yes, it might be obvious that your betrothed, who buys a new pair of shoes every time they go to the mall, is a Spender. Let them figure that out for themselves. *Do not* tell your spouse you already know exactly what Personality they have. Even if they keep money stuffed in a grocery bag at the back of the closet, don't tell them they're a Security Seeker. The discovery should be personal. Nothing feels worse than having someone else decide who you are.

The only way to build a solid Money Relationship is for both of you to know and accept your and your spouse's Money Personalities, and that can't happen unless you both take the time to understand your perspectives. Instead of ending up in a thirty-minute fight, send your spouse to our website (TheMoneyCouple.com or 5MoneyPersonalities. com) to take a ten-minute quiz and discover their Money Personality. Then you're ready to keep reading!

A Crowded Marriage

Once you and your spouse have identified your Primary and Secondary Money Personalities, take a minute to write them out and make a little chart like we did earlier. We'll use ourselves as an example to show what we mean.

	taylor	megan
1 PRIMARY	SPENDER	SAVER
2 SECONDARY	RISK TAKER	SECURITY SEEKER

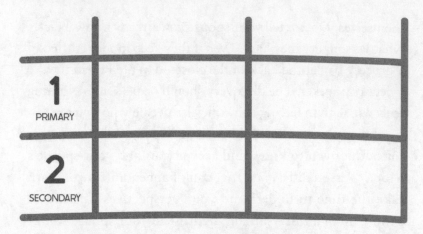

Now take a minute to fill in and look at your chart.

Can you see it? It's your Money Relationship in a nutshell. Seeing your Money Personalities laid out like this is a revelation, a major "wow" moment. For the first time, you can see why those little disagreements about money seem to turn into major arguments. Look at all those Money Personalities at work!

This chart is kind of a map for your Money Relationship. It shows you what you're dealing with. We've known about our Money Personalities for a long time, but the first time we wrote them out like this, it was a huge moment of discovery. We'd never really thought about the fact that there are *four* different Money Personalities at work in our relationship and that, at any given time, those combinations are interacting and bumping into each other in ways we had never understood before.

Sometimes we're the Spender and the Saver. Sometimes we're the Risk Taker and the Security Seeker. Sometimes we're the Spender and the Security Seeker or the Risk Taker and Saver. Now that you know a little more about the five Money Personalities, you can probably guess where we run into potential conflict. We can go shopping for Christmas gifts for the kids and have a perfect outing—spending the amount Megan has budgeted while still fulfilling my (Taylor's) desire to buy a ton of presents. On the ride home, when I tell Megan that I couldn't resist and got each kid something that wasn't on the list, my Spender tendencies square off against Megan's Security Seeker side.

If it sounds as though we have multiple personalities in our house, it's because we do. Before you judge us, remember that you have multiple personalities as well. We've spoken with countless couples, and we have yet to meet one where both spouses have the exact same Primary and Secondary Money Personalities. When it comes to money, opposites really do attract.

Naturally, that can create tension in a relationship. We'll look at that issue closer in the next chapter. For now, we want you to sit with this idea of multiple Money Personalities. Think about the implications for your relationship. Sure, there's potential for conflict, but there's just as much potential for maximizing the strengths of your various personalities. Not just in terms of your finances, but in your relationship in general.

Learning the Language

Knowing your Money Personality gives you huge insight into why you think the way you do about money. Knowing your spouse's Money Personality gives you huge insight into your spouse. Isn't that what makes a relationship hum? An intimate understanding of each other and what makes the other person tick?

That's why there's more to your Money Relationship than your financial plans. Every time you make a decision, you're bringing your perspective on life to the table. Few things feel better than making decisions with someone who understands and respects your perspective.

If you've ever traveled to a place where the locals don't speak the same language as you, you know how frustrating it can be to try to bridge the language barrier. Then when you finally find someone who speaks your language, it's a giant relief. You instantly feel heard and understood and can finally find the directions to the nearest bathroom!

The same thing happens when you and your spouse understand each other's Money Personalities. It's as though you've learned how to speak the same language. Now you can communicate and make your spouse feel heard, loved, and respected. I (Megan) know Taylor is always willing to take risks with our money. He knows those risky decisions can make me nervous. When he tells me about an investment opportunity that clearly has him excited and I smile through the anxiety and say, "Let's go for it!", I'm speaking his language. It's a way to show I appreciate and love him. When it comes time to focus on our savings, he's that much more likely to cater to my needs.

It took us a long time to get to the point where we understood each other well enough to really listen when the other person expressed any kind of fear or anxiety or frustration about a financial decision. By getting to know each other within the context of our Money Personalities, we've added a whole new level of trust and closeness to our relationship. We're absolutely certain the same can happen for you.

Walk a Mile

If you're struggling to understand your spouse's Money Personality, we want to suggest a simple, maybe even fun, exercise. Take a day for each of you and try to live out your spouse's Money Personality. No being snarky or mocking— "Hey, look at me, I'm buying stuff with money we don't have because I'm a Spender!" This has to be an honest attempt to learn something new about the person you married.

Some upcoming weekend, have one of you take Saturday and one of you take Sunday. Then go about your day, but have the assigned person talk out loud about the money decisions they are making. Let's look at a couple where one of them is a Spender and one is a Saver, a la the two of us. On Saturday they're both going to live like the Spender. Here's how that day might look:

They wake up and get dressed for the day. The Spender looks in his closet and says, "Okay, when I look at my wardrobe, I see a bunch of stuff I'm tired of wearing. I like to feel good about how I look, so my first thought when I get dressed is that I could really use some new shirts. Then I start thinking about when I can go shopping, and I buy them."

The Saver's heart is starting to race at the idea that her

spouse is *already* thinking about spending money and they haven't even left the bedroom. However, because this couple is committed to understanding each other and healing their Money Relationship, she sits on the edge of the bed and listens. She might even say, in the kindest way possible, "Wow, honey, I had no idea you started thinking about spending money so early in the day."

The Spender is then likely to suggest going out for brunch, because why not? This will cause the Saver's blood pressure to rise once more, but love will take over once again, and the Saver will go along with the idea. As this couple moves through their day, the Spender is going to keep talking about what he's thinking and why he's thinking it. The Saver is going to listen and do everything she can to learn about her beloved's perspective.

On Sunday it's the Saver's turn. Now when the couple wakes up, the Saver might say, "It's kind of cold in here, but I like that—it means we're not running up the heating bill as much as we did last winter." The Spender, in turn, has to keep his lips zipped and discover the inner workings of his spouse's Saver identity.

They'll go through the morning, with the couple making more decisions that involve money. Will they grab coffee on the way to church? How much should they put in the collection plate? How many brownies will they buy to support the youth group's bake sale? Through it all the Saver will talk her husband through her thought process on every one of these choices. By lunchtime the Spender is going to be amazed at how heavily money decisions weigh on his lovely Saver.

We want to be clear: we're not telling you to go out and spend money you don't have or to give your spouse free rein to destroy your finances in a day. If you'd rather make hypothetical decisions, that's fine. You could say something like, "If we went into your favorite store right now, what would you do first?" The point of this exercise is to build understanding and even a bit of respect for your spouse's Money Personality, and you can do that without spending a cent.

For so many couples, their Money Relationship is a tangle of false assumptions, old resentments, and constant blame. At the root of all of that is a misunderstanding of who the other person is and why they behave the way they do. When these couples discover their Money Personalities and take the time to really understand each other, they begin to see past those assumptions and resentments. That's when they can see what's really happening in their Money Relationship.

Seeing What's Real

That chart you filled out earlier in this chapter? We call it the *Big Reveal* because it uncovers the underlying dynamics at work in your Money Relationship. When viewed the wrong way, it's easy to use this information to start placing blame and criticizing your spouse. At our conferences when we address large groups of couples and do the Big Reveal, we see most of them exchange a look that says, *Now we know who's causing the problems. It's you!*

We'd like you to flip that idea on its head. Instead of

using this information as a weapon to chastise your spouse, use it as a tool to rebuild a better Money Relationship. Use it to deal with the realities of your relationship instead of the assumptions and labels and fears you've been harboring. When you do, you can repair years of pain and relational damage.

Fred and Heidi came to one of our seminars with a long history of money conflict. They told us this seminar was their last-ditch effort to solve their money problems and avoid getting a divorce. Needless to say, the pressure was on during this meeting. We took them through the Money Personality Profile and found out that they had four of the five Money Personalities in their relationship. Heidi was a Saver/Risk Taker and Fred was a Spender/Flyer.

It turned out that Heidi controlled their finances because she was afraid Fred would spend all their money. She needed that money on hand to keep her small business afloat, so she essentially gave Fred an allowance.

Fred, on the other hand, had a bank account left over from his bachelor days that Heidi didn't know about. He didn't really intend to use it once they got married, but he never got around to closing it. When Heidi started talking about how much money she needed for her business, Fred started putting money in his secret account just to have a little backup in case Heidi's plans fell apart.

There was a lot of anger and mistrust in this relationship. Fred told Heidi she was a control freak. Heidi was livid about Fred keeping secrets. We got them calm enough to take the Money Personality Profile, and while it didn't solve all their problems, it did serve as a revelation. It turned out that Fred had deep-seated fears that Heidi would use up all their money, and Heidi acknowledged that he wasn't just being overly paranoid—her business was risky, and it was a good idea to keep some of their money out of it. Fred admitted that he was wrong not to trust Heidi with their money; she was a savvy businesswoman and had made them a lot of money with her risky investments. It was the insight they needed to turn their relationship around.

If you want to fix your Money Relationship, you have to be honest with yourself and your spouse and know what's real. You have to break out of the cycle of blame and start seeing the situation from your spouse's point of view (see the Appendix for *The Five Money Personalities Survival Guide*), and the only way to do that is to know each other's Money Personalities. When you do, you can start to see why your spouse makes the decisions they make. You can see the ways their Money Personality has helped your family. You can appreciate the time and effort and thought that goes into your spouse's money decisions. You can start to extend grace to your spouse during times that would have pulled you apart in the past.

When you let this happen, you might find that you've begun to heal far more than just your Money Relationship. In some ways, all of this work is like going back to those early days of dating—the days when there was no one as fascinating to you as your sweetheart. You wanted to know everything about each other—her favorite flower, his favorite kind of socks, the story behind that scar. No detail was too mundane, no story too silly. It was important and interesting because it was part of this person you loved.

Very often, soon after people get married, they tend to stop discovering each other. We get to that place of familiarity and forget that our spouses are deep wells of quirks, dreams, and ideas that are still worth unearthing. Let the work you're doing on your Money Personalities feed your interest in your spouse. Let it reinvigorate your curiosity about this unique and special person you married. Even if he's been driving you nuts with his spending, even if she's making you crazy with her coupons, try to look at the person behind those behaviors and find that sweetheart who, not so long ago, was everything to you.

At the beginning of this book, we talked about how important it is for couples to dream together. We know how quickly daily life can steal the dreams you had when you first got together. It might feel like the dreams of your future and your family and the places you'd go and the things you'd do have drifted away, but we promise you can get them back. Understanding your Money Personalities is like a deposit in the dream bank. It's a solid step forward on the road to a better Money Relationship and a better marriage.

Make It Happen

OVER the next week, try to make three decisions about money as though you had your spouse's Money Personality. Over dinner, talk about what you learned during the experiment.

SIX

Opposites Attract

KAREN and Jamal started dating when they were in their late twenties. Jamal had a great job with a law firm, and Karen was in grad school. Karen loved Jamal's sense of adventure, his free spirit, and his generous heart. He would treat total strangers to a coffee on his morning java run and spend his weekends hiking and exploring new places. He also loved to surprise Karen with gifts, like a scarf she'd been eyeing or flowers in the middle of winter—and eventually a stunning diamond engagement ring.

Jamal loved Karen's sense of purpose, her drive to make the world a better place. She worked hard and focused intensely on everything she did. He loved her commitment to her friends, her family, and her work. He loved that she had big ideas about her future, and he wanted to be a part of those plans. She was like a steady ship in the sometimes-chaotic seas of Jamal's life.

Things were almost perfect. And then they got married.

It wasn't long before Jamal and Karen found themselves with very different ideas about how to handle their money. Jamal wanted to take Karen on a post-graduation trip to India. He thought it would be a great way to celebrate her accomplishments. Karen knew it would only be a few months before she had to start paying back her student loans, and she wanted to get a jump start on saving money so they could pay off the debt in three years.

They were still in the newlywed phase when they hit a wall of misunderstanding and blame. Karen thought Jamal was living in a dreamland and that he needed to start being more responsible with their money. Jamal thought Karen was a stick-in-the-mud who worried too much about their bank account.

That's the version where couples discover their issues early on. On the opposite end of the spectrum, we've got Linda and Ted.

They'd been married for nearly thirty-five years when their Money Relationship exploded. For most of their marriage, Ted had worked, and Linda had stayed home with their three kids. Linda wasn't interested in their finances; they had more than enough to cover their expenses, and that was all she needed to know.

Ted and Linda had been high school sweethearts. They got married when they were both twenty and essentially grew up together. They had highly defined roles in their relationship, and they both liked it that way. From the day she met him, Linda loved Ted's strength and the way he took care of her and, years later, the children. He was kind, decisive, and smart, but he also had just enough of a wild side to make their lives together an adventure. He taught Linda how to ski, how to fish, how to build a campfire, and how to shoot a basket. He made her feel protected, cared for, and loved.

Ted was attracted to Linda from the get-go. She was sweet, funny, and thoughtful. When they were teenagers, she'd bake him cookies, cheer for him from the bleachers, and listen patiently when he was disappointed in a grade or the outcome of a game. He could be a little over the top sometimes, but Linda helped him feel grown-up and smart. She seemed to see the best in him, and that felt great.

While Ted was in college, Linda juggled three jobs to help keep them afloat. Once he graduated, he promised her she'd never have to work another day in her life, and he made sure to keep that promise by taking a secure job with an insurance agency, one where he knew he could make a good living and take care of his growing family.

Decades later things changed without warning. Ted came home in the middle of the day and told Linda he was about to be laid off. As bad as that news was, the situation was actually much worse. He confessed that he hadn't been honest with her about their finances. He had tapped into their retirement account years earlier to help pay off their mounting debt. He'd hoped to work another ten years to make up the difference, but now he didn't know what to do. He didn't know if he would be able to find another job, certainly not one that paid what he'd been making. With the undisclosed spending, they didn't have the savings needed to weather a season of unemployment.

Needless to say, Linda was stunned. As they talked, Ted

came clean about his mistakes with their money, mistakes that had left them in danger of losing their house and nearly everything Linda thought was safe and secure.

After her initial shock wore off, Linda was, understandably, livid. How could he keep this from her? Why didn't he include her in these decisions? Why did he wait until it was too late to come to her? Ted confessed that he'd never told her about any of this because he didn't want to worry her. He knew she'd trusted him to take care of her, and instead he'd made decisions that could destroy their marriage.

Young or old, high school sweethearts or recently eloped, we hear stories like this all the time. Two people meet and fall in love. In those early days their differences are what bring them together; but once they have a few years and a whole lot of money decisions under their belts, those qualities that were so attractive when they were dating have become a source of conflict in their marriage. Sometimes it's an obvious clash, as it was for Jamal and Karen. Sometimes it's lurking just beneath the surface, only to erupt like it did for Linda and Ted.

We have found that roughly 90 percent of the couples we work with have an Opposite Dynamic in their relationship. That doesn't surprise us one bit. There's something subconscious in the way we are drawn to the opposite Money Personality. We recognize that this other person will add something important to our lives. A Security Seeker might be drawn to the Risk Taker because the Risk Taker brings the thrill of the unknown into the Security Seeker's predictable life. A Spender might be drawn to a Saver's sense of responsibility and stability. A Saver might be drawn to a Flyer's generosity. Whatever it is, it seems that when it comes to Money Personalities, the old adage we alluded to earlier is right: opposites do attract.

Bring Back the Attraction

A strong marriage is only possible when couples reclaim that attraction, when they stop seeing the downsides of their differences and start loving the way they complement each other. The only way to create this attraction resurgence is to take an honest look at how your Money Personalities affect your Money Relationship.

Remember the Opposite Dynamic from chapter 4? On one side of the scale we have the Spender, the Risk Taker, and the Flyer. On the other side we have the Saver and the Security Seeker.

Many of us have the Opposite Dynamic in ourselves. Our Primary Money Personality is on one side of the scale, and our Secondary Money Personality is on the other side. The same thing naturally happens in couples, like with us. Our journey—finding attraction in our opposition, then dealing with the resulting conflict, and finally recognizing how much strength we gained from our differences—is what makes this issue so important and personal.

The vast majority of the people we work with have the Opposite Dynamic in their relationship, and it doesn't surprise us when that contrast causes conflict. Take Joe and Ann, for example.

In the Big Reveal their Money Personalities look like this:

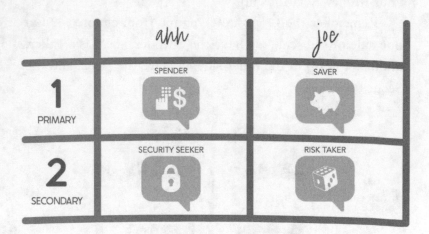

They have four of the five Money Personalities at work in their Money Relationship. That's a lot of potential collisions.

For the most part Joe and Ann have a strong relationship. Still, the little differences between them are starting to add up and are causing increased tension in their marriage.

That's because every decision they make involves their competing Money Personalities.

- Ann wants to go skiing over the holiday break. Joe is happy to stay home and have a staycation.
- Ann wants to try out a new restaurant. Joe wants to stick with the value menu at their neighborhood burger place.
- Joe is thinking about starting a small business. Ann is scared they'll lose their hard-earned savings.

The Opposite Dynamic in Ann and Joe's relationship means they see the world through very different lenses. With so many discrepancies, the money decisions are wearing them down as a couple.

Because every couple has as many as four Money Personalities at work, the Opposite Dynamic adds an interesting layer of complexity to your Money Relationship. To make things easier to process, we've put together a simple method for figuring out how many Opposite Dynamics you have in your relationship. Once you know the answer, you'll be able to see just where the tension might be coming from in a conflict about money.

Here's how to figure it out:

1. Go back to the results of your Big Reveal in chapter 5.
2. Starting in the top left corner and moving clockwise, count every instance of the Opposite Dynamic.

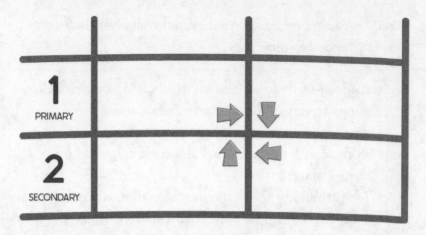

Ann and Joe's Opposite Dynamic would look like this:

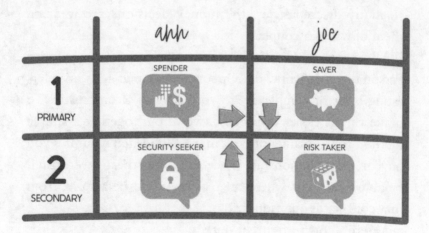

As you can see, Ann and Joe have four Opposite Dynamics in their relationship:

- Between Spender and Saver = 1
- Between Saver and Risk Taker = 1

- Between Risk Taker and Security Seeker = 1
- Between Security Seeker and Spender = 1
- Total: 4

There's no right or wrong number of Opposite Dynamics. We have two in our relationship, and it doesn't make us any more or less prone to conflict than other couples. What matters isn't the number but your awareness of these potential areas of disagreement and misunderstanding. Knowing where you see things a bit differently can go a long way toward helping you make money decisions with care and kindness.

Once Joe and Ann discovered that they have four Opposite Dynamics in their marriage, they could see that their arguments about money weren't really about money at all. Their argument about where to go on vacation had nothing to do with the merits of skiing versus the joys of staying home. It was about Ann wanting to do something fun and Joe feeling that they couldn't afford to take an expensive vacation at that time. Once they got to the heart of the matter, Joe agreed it would be nice to get out of town but suggested a week at a cabin a few hours away where they could cross-country ski for half the price of a trip to the mountains. Ann loved the idea, Joe set a budget, and they did some research and found the perfect place.

Choosing a restaurant stopped turning into a fight and became a chance for them to break some bad habits. Instead of going out to eat because they didn't feel like cooking, they decided to splurge on a couple of great meals each month rather than eating at the most convenient place twice a week. Ann's Spender Personality got to indulge a bit while Joe's Saver Personality could feel good about reducing their eating out expenses. Best of all, with the option of a quick bite at a restaurant off the table, they discovered they liked making simple meals together at home. As a Risk Taker, Joe loved to try new recipes, and Ann was happy to be his guinea pig.

The small business Joe hoped to start had been a real point of contention for these two. It pushed all of Ann's Security Seeker buttons, and for a long time she was not willing to budge on her refusal to free up money for this risky endeavor. After talking through their Opposite Dynamics, Ann decided she was willing to keep talking about it. It was still too big a leap for her to just say yes, but she no longer refused to consider the possibility. For Joe and Ann, being able to move this conversation from "too hot to handle" to "let's keep talking it through" was a huge step in the right direction.

Seeing the ways in which the Opposite Dynamic plays out in your marriage isn't a free ticket to no more conflict. It's a way to recognize that those conflicts don't have to get personal or painful. You can address problems as partners, not as adversaries, because you know that the other person is coming at the issue from a legitimate perspective that just happens to be different from yours. When you understand that, you can work through problems with respect and a true desire to find middle ground.

We're often asked if there is a Money Personality combination that just doesn't work, and we always give the same answer: no. The differences in your Money Personalities are never insurmountable, not if you're both committed to understanding and respecting each other and willing to remember what it was about those differences that attracted you in the first place. After all, if we can find strength in our Opposite Dynamic, anyone can.

It isn't the differences between you and your spouse that create tension in your Money Relationship. It's the nitpicking, the controlling, and the assuming that cause problems. The good news is that you can change that. You can change the way you talk to each other and the way you make decisions. It's all about finding the strengths in your Money Relationship.

Stronger Together

Just as your personal Opposite Dynamic helps you keep your Money Personalities in check, the Opposite Dynamic in your relationship can be a huge advantage. As a Saver/ Security Seeker and a Spender/Risk Taker, Megan and I (Taylor) view money through entirely different lenses. If I decided mine was the only way to approach finances, I'd be frustrated constantly. By finding the value in her perspective, I've grown without having to sacrifice. I also feel like I'm a lot more organized than I otherwise would be.

The Spender side of me has never been shy. I had no trouble burning through money I didn't have before Megan and I got serious, and allowing myself to get advice from a Saver/Security Seeker was one of the best things I ever did. I don't feel controlled or stifled by her caution; in fact, I feel more empowered by it. As long as I keep enough money in the bank to help her sleep easy at night, I can take risks and spend money and still feel like a good husband and father.

Megan recognizes the urges I have as a Spender, and while she doesn't try to talk me out of them, she forces me to at least think through my half-baked ideas. If I can convince her an investment is good, I get her blessing. If I can't convince her, there's a good chance it's because the investment isn't airtight.

There was a time when we hadn't discovered or identified our Money Personalities and these conversations were a lot harder to have. We didn't understand where the other was coming from, so even the slightest bit of pushback felt combative. Now I know Megan wants to feel confident before signing a check, and she understands how I take calculated risks.

We also know that the other's initial reaction to a money decision isn't the final position. We take the time to listen to each other and discuss our options, all the while making sure to respect the other's needs. Megan needs to know I won't buy stock in a start-up unless she's on board, and I need to feel like she'll at least hear me out before offering a dissenting opinion.

What's more, we've learned that we make far better decisions together than either of us would make on our own. If I weren't there to push Megan forward, she'd have mountains of money that she was too afraid to spend. If I didn't have her as a voice of reason and measured encouragement, I might own a bunch of snow cone stands in North Dakota!

It wasn't easy for us to get to this point. We've had plenty of serious arguments about money, and I'm sure there are more on the horizon. Even so, there have been far fewer than before we started communicating, and the ones that *do* arise come and go much quicker and without any long-term harm.

It's so easy to think of your spouse's Money Personality as a giant *NO* stamped on your dreams. Spenders can feel hemmed in by their Saver spouses, while Spenders make those same Savers feel like their lives are out of control. The Risk Taker feels limited, the Security Seeker feels threatened, and the Flyer feels trapped. Those sentiments are natural, but as long as you're willing to shift your perspective and see your partner's Money Personality as an asset in your Money Relationship, you'll find yourselves moving forward with the belief that you are stronger together than you can ever be apart.

WE HAVE FOUND THAT **75%** OF ALL COUPLES MARRY THEIR MONEY OPPOSITE!

Make It Happen

THINK about the ways your Money
Personalities combine with your spouse's.
Now answer these questions:

1. How many Opposite Dynamics does your
   relationship have?
2. What challenges do your opposite
   Money Personalities create in your Money
   Relationship?
3. What are some ways you can use
   Opposite Dynamics to make better
   decisions together?
4. Finally, tell your spouse one thing
   you appreciate about their Money
   Personalities.

PART 2

THE HEART OF
THE MATTER

SEVEN

Your Money or Your Wife

IF your financial picture were the only thing at stake in your Money Relationship, we wouldn't be writing this book. There are plenty of resources out there to help you put together a balanced budget or get out of debt or invest well. By now you know that in our opinion, your budget, your debt, and your investments are not the real issues in your relationship. What's at stake is not your money; it's your marriage.

If it were just about the money, it wouldn't hurt so much when your wife says you're cheap. You wouldn't be so angry when your husband spends more on groceries than you'd budgeted. You wouldn't feel so ignored when your partner starts a business even though the risk scares you to death.

But it *does* hurt. We *do* get angry. We *can* feel ignored.

Because it's not about the money.

We worked with a couple who had a great plan for saving money. They each had a small cookie tin on top of the fridge, and the idea was they'd put a little spending money in their tins each week and then get to use it however they wanted. She had her tin, he had his.

The husband was a golfer and had his eye on a high-end driver. He saved his spending money for months to buy this golf club. Finally, he knew he had enough to make the purchase. That weekend, he pulled his tin down from the fridge, opened it up, and found . . . that it was empty.

He went to his wife and asked her if she knew what had happened to his money. She said, "Oh, I used it." He didn't even have the words to ask her what she'd used it for. It didn't matter what the answer was. It didn't matter that he could save his money again and get his driver in a few months. He told us, "I felt like she'd cheated on me." It wasn't the loss of the money that hurt; it was the loss of trust in his wife that left him devastated. They'd had a deal, and she ignored it. She intentionally broke their pledge. That's what hurt.

This was the story that convinced us that there is something profoundly painful about the ways in which couples hurt each other when it comes to money. It's serious enough that we started calling this kind of behavior *financial infidelity*.

Are You Cheating?

We use the term *financial infidelity* to refer to a host of money-related behavior: lying about money, hiding money, secretly hoarding money, or just about anything that involves one spouse being less than honest with the other as it relates to finances.

In all our meetings, classes, and seminars, we have yet to meet a couple who has zero financial infidelity in their relationship. We have it, you have it, everyone has it. While we hear lots of stories of terrible, blatant financial infidelity, it isn't always intentional. It isn't always a huge, devastating secret. In fact, most cases of financial infidelity are relatively innocent.

Sometimes it doesn't even involve much money. Maybe you tell your spouse you spent "about fifty bucks" on a birthday present when you really spent $75. That might not seem like a big deal, and maybe from a purely financial perspective it isn't, but it's still a dishonest statement regarding the money you spent.

Financial infidelity is far more pervasive and complex than we once thought. We've found that 65 percent of women have a secret credit card or a secret stash of cash. Before any of you guys start getting suspicious of your wives, you need to hear the next part. The majority of these women said they set up these accounts because they were concerned about their family's finances. They worried about their husband's reckless spending and didn't trust him to make good financial decisions on their behalf.

Guys, still thinking about confronting your wife?

Financial infidelity, like sexual infidelity, usually starts out with a small breach of trust. It's like the office affair that starts with conversations around the watercooler, then turns into lunch, then turns into dinner, then turns into a sexual relationship.

With financial infidelity, it's the same snowball effect. You say you're going to spend $100, but you end up spending $200. You keep a little secret stash of cash in your underwear drawer, a stash that goes from $50 to $100 to $500 to $5,000, and you never tell your spouse about it.

The biggest form of financial infidelity, and which causes the most lasting damage in a relationship, is meant to be hurtful. It's the secret credit cards with big balances, the intentional lies about spending, the total control over finances, the undisclosed bank account. That's the stuff that pushes marriages to the brink of divorce—and beyond.

It's Not About the Money

The emotional toll of financial infidelity is far more devastating than the toll it takes on your money. You can figure out how to recover from overspending. You can find a way to get some money put away for retirement. You can work through almost any money problem if you put in the effort. It takes an entirely different approach to recover from the loss of trust that comes from financial infidelity.

We know a couple who ended up divorced after the wife discovered her husband had run up tens of thousands of dollars in debt on a secret credit card. Even though it was a big financial setback, it wasn't the debt that pushed her to leave him. She didn't care about that nearly as much as she cared about the breakdown in their communication, trust, and life partnership.

Financial infidelity hurts because it goes to the heart of

a couple's commitment to each other. It's a breach of trust, a sign of indifference, a lack of respect. That relational erosion always hurts, no matter how much money is involved.

As sad as this section feels, we have seen a lot of couples heal from the pain of financial infidelity. We've seen them agree to put an end to lies and control and secrets and start over again. We've seen couples who were emotionally bankrupt start reinvesting in their relationship and rebuilding the dreams and plans that had brought them together in the first place. It takes patience, grace, and a tremendous commitment to break old habits, but you can *Make It Happen*.

There's a little financial infidelity in every relationship, and in the next chapter we're going to help you get to the root causes of this persistent, universal problem. In order to put an end to it, you need to start by learning how it worked its way into your Money Relationship to start with.

We have put together something we call the Money Relationship Assessment (MRA), and you can find it at TheMoneyCouple.com. Before you read the next chapter, use the MRA to measure the amount of financial infidelity in your relationship. It's best if you and your spouse each take it separately and talk about your scores *after* you've finished this book. In other words, you aren't going to reveal your scores to each other right now. You're taking the MRA so that each of you can get a clear look at what's going on in your Money Relationship.

It's absolutely essential that you are brutally honest on the MRA. You can't heal what's broken in your Money Relationship unless you face it. Answer the questions as truthfully as you can, ignoring the tiny voice in your head that urges you to fudge the numbers a little. We're going to give you a guide on how to talk through your results with your spouse, so don't stress about that part. Instead, take a deep breath and get ready to put an end to the secrets and lies and deceptions that have the potential to destroy your Money Relationship and your marriage.

Please keep in mind that your score isn't a sign of how close you are to divorce. The fact that you're on chapter 7 of this book means you're serious about changing the direction of your Money Relationship. Your score will give you a good picture of where you are and where to focus your efforts as you work through the remaining chapters.

Make It Happen

GO to TheMoneyCouple.com and fill out the Money Relationship Assessment. Does your score surprise you? Are there things you do that you never thought of as infidelity? What can you do to be more honest in your Money Relationship?

EIGHT

The Roots of Financial Infidelity

THE point of uncovering financial infidelity in your Money Relationship isn't to point fingers or to place blame. It's to help you and your spouse understand what's really happening in your relationship so that you can get rid of everything that's holding you back from a strong, healthy marriage.

In the same way that understanding your Money Personalities helps you and your spouse stop assuming the worst about each other, understanding how and why financial infidelity creeps into a relationship will allow you to name it and deal with it. That's how you get the trust back. That's how you grow closer as a couple. That's how you reclaim all those dreams you had.

The MRA will give you a score that lets you know how much financial infidelity exists in your relationship. It won't, however, tell you what that financial infidelity is really all about or how to fix it. That's what we're going to cover in the next few chapters.

There are five main reasons couples commit financial infidelity:

1. Financial Separation
2. Overspending and Debt
3. Lack of Planning
4. Control
5. Money Secrets

Whether you have a lot of financial infidelity or a little, whether it's intentional or accidental, it's crucial to understand why it happens and how you can keep it from destroying your marriage. Let's look at the five main reasons in more detail.

Financial Separation

Whenever we start talking to a group about financial separation as the cause of financial infidelity, we almost always see a hand shoot up in the audience: "Are you saying it's wrong to have separate checking accounts?" Short answer to that question: no.

We don't have a problem with separate checking accounts. There are plenty of good reasons to have them. Maybe you have one for personal use and one for business use. Perhaps you've got one for his expenses, one for hers, and one for both. You can have twenty-five checking accounts, fifteen credit cards, and four savings accounts for all we care. As long as both parties are *transparent* with what is coming in and going out of those accounts, the separation isn't a problem.

A couple years back, we were in the airport waiting for a flight. There was a couple who looked to be in their sixties sitting behind us at the gate. They were in the middle of a heated conversation, and we couldn't help but overhear them. Evidently she had some bank account that was separate from his. She had put a significant amount of money into this account, something to the tune of $100,000. Her husband was furious.

> HIM: I don't know anything about this bank or these people. Why didn't you just put it in the other account?
>
> HER: I didn't think it should go there. It needed to be in this account.
>
> HIM: But I don't know this bank at all. Who are these people?
>
> HER: It's not a problem. It's going to be fine there.
>
> HIM: You don't know that. I want to talk to someone at this bank.

The more they talked, the more we could see that the problem was that she had made a decision without him. He didn't have any real reason not to trust the bank she'd chosen—it was a national bank he'd likely heard of—but he didn't like that she'd gone ahead and deposited a huge amount of their money in a new place without consulting him. It wasn't what she'd done that bothered him; it's that she'd done it without him. That felt like financial infidelity.

Her reactions suggested that she was irritated at his seeming lack of trust in her decision. She wanted him to trust her judgment, but he didn't. For her, his need to control her decisions felt like financial infidelity.

Again, we don't have a problem with couples having separate checking accounts. If you and your spouse have them, you just need to take extra care to avoid the appearance of financial infidelity. These arrangements can be a minefield of mistrust and misunderstanding.

No matter how much money is in your separate accounts, no matter why you have them, it's crucial that you have 100 percent transparency in your communication about those accounts. Both you and your spouse should know exactly how much money is going into and out of those accounts and why. As long as you're both fully aware of the various places money is getting deposited and withdrawn, separate accounts shouldn't be a problem.

What *is* a problem is separation for the sake of secrecy or security. If you have a separate credit card because you don't want your spouse to know about it, you're committing financial infidelity. If you have a separate checking account because you don't trust your spouse with your money, you're committing financial infidelity. We find that every Money Personality can be tempted to keep some money separate from the family finances. Savers want to know they have a little cushion; Spenders like to have a stash that no one else can control; Security Seekers want to protect their nest eggs; Risk Takers want liquid funds they can access quickly; and Flyers don't mean to keep their money separate, but they might forget they still have money in a checking account in the town where they went to college. In other words, all of us can be sucked into financial infidelity.

Maintaining separate finances is like having separate date nights. They might be convenient, but they don't help you grow closer as a couple. They are a sign that there's some doubt and a lack of partnership. When there's a lack of trust and cohesiveness in a relationship, financial infidelity is much more likely to worm its way in.

Overspending and Debt

So many couples struggle with spending and debt, especially those of us who are Spenders and Risk Takers. It can stem from a sense of financial entitlement. We tell ourselves we deserve those golf clubs, that new dress, that boat. We work hard and want to enjoy the fruits of our labors.

For couples of all income levels, debt can tear a relationship apart. We know couples who, through nothing more than a spending spree or two, found themselves deep in debt only a few months into their marriages. Once that debt is there, other dreams immediately hit the shelves as interest eats away at earnings. You can't buy a house because your credit score is shot. You can't have a baby because you can't move into a bigger house. You can't change jobs or go back to school or travel because every cent gets sucked away by creditors.

One couple needed furniture for their first apartment and, in the throes of wedding spending, furnished their living room, bedroom, and dining room with brand new tables, chairs, a couch, dressers, a bed, end tables, nightstands, and a buffet. When the bill arrived, they were stunned to realize they had accrued several thousand dollars in debt they couldn't quickly pay back. They'd figured this was how every couple started out, but a few conversations with friends showed them they had made a very expensive mistake. Ten years into their marriage, they continue to pay off that debt, not to mention student loans, car payments, and additional credit card spending that happened as a result of the first furnishing splurge. Their dreams of owning a home have been pushed back so far it hardly enters the conversation anymore.

The stress of debt can leave couples open to financial infidelity. They agree to cut back, but the Spender can't resist that new video game or those cute shoes. They are living paycheck to paycheck, but the Risk Taker will use one of those paychecks as an investment in his buddy's new business. That's when the secrets start; that's when they start lying about their spending, hiding receipts, or borrowing money to cover their mistakes. It's an ugly, vicious cycle.

Lack of Planning

We see this come up in older couples we work with, people who are ready to send their kids to college or are nearing retirement. They get to the point where they need a pretty decent chunk of money and it just isn't there.

Remember the story we told you at the beginning of the book about the couple getting a divorce after more than forty years of marriage? Their issue was lack of planning. She was a Security Seeker, and he was a Flyer. For years she'd been anxious about their retirement, asking him to put more aside for the future, and he'd let it go. The closer they got to retirement age, the more anxious she became until she couldn't deal with it anymore and left him.

Other couples find themselves caught unprepared for the future and get angry at each other. They start blaming each other and trying desperately to solve the problem. One of them might sell off a car or even the house in hopes of bringing in money. The Risk Taker might throw all the couple's savings into one last-ditch investment in an effort to come up with more money. The Security Seeker will be so freaked out they will shut down emotionally. The whole relationship starts to fall apart from the stress.

Lately we've been meeting with an increasing number of couples who are struggling to help their kids pay for college. In many cases they had good intentions to start some sort of savings plan, but time flies by, tuition keeps going up, and they are suddenly faced with a difficult choice: sacrifice their own financial situation to help pay for school, or ask their kids to take out loans that will leave them with huge debt before they even have a chance to join the workforce. There is no good solution in these cases, only the lesser of two lousy choices.

The desperation of these situations often leads to plenty of accusations and blame. Carol and Neil will send their oldest daughter off to college in another year, and Carol is panicked. They haven't saved a dime for her education. The topic came up when their daughter was in elementary school, but Neil thought it was pointless. He figured their daughter was going to have to take out loans no matter how much they saved, so they might as well enjoy that money while they had it.

Carol never agreed with this approach, but she didn't want to keep having the same argument, so eventually she stopped bringing it up. Now that their daughter is a junior in high school, years' worth of nerves are coming to a head. Carol had to pay her own way through college, which left her with a lot of student loans, and she doesn't want her daughter to deal with that same burden. The arguing stopped years ago, but Carol's anger at the situation never went away.

Because of the resentment and assumptions, Carol is taking matters into her own hands. Without Neil knowing, she met with their bank to look into taking out her own loan so she could absorb the debt instead of their daughter. She looked at the Blue Book value of their cars to see if they could free up some money by selling a vehicle and getting something cheaper. If Neil won't help, Carol is prepared to handle the situation herself.

Now that it's crunch time, Neil feels about the same way he's always felt. He's counting on loans, grants, and work-study to cover their daughter's tuition. He doesn't understand what Carol is so worked up about. He knows plenty of other parents who put their money into retirement instead of college with the idea that it will be easier for their kids to pay off student loans now than to have to support their aging parents later. He wants his kids to learn that you have to work for your education—that it means more when you've earned it yourself instead of having it handed to you by your parents.

Neil and Carol are deeply entrenched in their own assessments and assumptions about the other's way of thinking. The lack of planning ten years ago has led Carol to a state of desperation, one that has all the hallmarks of financial infidelity.

Control

If one person takes control of all the money, you can guarantee there will be financial infidelity in the relationship. We have a client who called one day all fired up. "We need to come in and see you," he said. "I just found a $12,000 balance on a credit card my wife had that I didn't know about. I'm so mad I don't know what to do."

We obliged, and they came in, the husband storming in first and his wife trailing behind him. He was all red in the face, and she was as calm as could be. We sat down and started looking over the credit card bill. As we looked, we didn't see the kinds of expenses we expected to see on a secret credit card—shopping trips, online purchases, travel expenses. Instead, it was trips to the grocery store, household supplies, school supplies, etc.

We asked her to explain the bill to us, and she went right down the list. "That was for extra food for a business dinner we hosted. That was for the kids' school clothes. That was my regular grocery store run." There wasn't anything on that bill that shouldn't have been covered by their regular budget. When we asked her why she had a secret card for that stuff, she said, "He doesn't give me enough money to cover these things."

Even though the husband had called the meeting, we had to give him the bad news. "This bill isn't her problem," we told him. "It's yours. You're controlling the finances so intensely that you don't let her spend what it takes to care for the daily needs of your family."

The more we dug into this couple's story, the clearer it became that he was a classic controller. He didn't believe she could handle the family finances, so he took charge of everything. He didn't trust her to be honest about her spending, so he gave her an allowance that let him keep track of every cent. He didn't talk to her about their money, so he had no idea what it really cost to manage a household.

This is a classic case of one spouse holding the purse strings so tightly that the other spouse is driven to commit financial infidelity by default. When that's happening, it's only a matter of time before that marriage is over. There is no trust, no respect, no partnership. Unless the controlling spouse is willing to let go and build a true Money Relationship, the marriage is done for.

Money Secrets

Money secrets take on a life of their own. One of our favorite stories involves an unintentional money secret. A client of ours told us about something that had happened to him a decade or so earlier. He had an opportunity to invest in a company that he was really excited about. He told his wife about it but then dismissed it because he knew they didn't have the $10,000 he needed to own a share in this business.

His wife looked at him and said, "Wait here." She ran into the bedroom and came back holding a brown grocery bag, then started pulling fistfuls of cash out of it. When emptied, she'd taken more than $12,000 out of that sack.

Her husband was understandably stunned. "Where did you get this?"

"It's my bra money," she answered. "My mother taught me this. Every time I go to the store, I write a check for $10 extra, put the money in my bra and bring it home. I've been doing it since we got married."

On the one hand, he was thrilled. At the same time, he was a little bothered that they had never talked about it. All that money, for all those years, and he'd never known about it.

In that case the money secret was a pretty good one. Most of the time, money secrets are disastrous. They bankrupt families and leave a trail of foreclosures, destroyed credit, and deep debt behind them. On top of that, and more importantly, they destroy relationships.

We've told you about some ugly financial infidelity here.

These examples might make it easy to feel like having a few little secrets now and then is no big deal compared to the couples with years of deception and control behind them. Here's the thing about financial infidelity: even a little bit can create big problems in your relationship. Just like a single grain of sand in your shoe can give you a painful blister on your foot, a tiny act of dishonesty can wear away the trust and respect that are crucial to a healthy Money Relationship.

Imagine a glass jar. The emptiness inside represents the whole of your marriage. Every time you commit financial infidelity, no matter how unintentional or how innocent, no matter how much or how little money is involved, it's like adding a handful of rocks to that jar. Every handful crowds out the good stuff that makes your marriage work.

The good news is that you can overcome financial infidelity. You can stop it, right now, and move forward by forgiving each other and building new patterns in your Money Relationship. In the next chapter we're going to teach you how to dump out all those rocks of resentment and anger and mistrust and control and replace them with the clean, pure air of communication and cooperation.

Make It Happen

IDENTIFY one of the five causes of financial infidelity that you've seen in your marriage. Now make one commitment that can help you end that deceit. For example, you can decide to talk about any purchase over $100 or agree to look over credit card statements together every month.

NINE

The Money Dump

HOW are you doing? We know that those last couple of chapters might have been painful, especially if you have a lot of financial infidelity in your relationship. In light of that, we want to remind you of the commitment you made at the very beginning of this book. You believed you had a relationship worth saving. In the journey to save your Money Relationship, that commitment makes all the difference.

We know that not every relationship can survive lies and secrets and years of resentment. However, we also know that when couples are willing to try something new, to break out of old patterns and learn new skills, they can rebuild their marriages. That's what the next few chapters are about. We're going to give you three tools that you can use from here on out to get your relationship back on track and start living out those dreams that have slipped away.

A strong Money Relationship doesn't just happen. It takes

some serious work, but we think the effort can still be kind of fun. We've designed these three tools—the Money Dump; the Money Huddle; and the Stop, Drop, and Roll Guide to Fighting Fair—to be easy to remember and easy to fit into your busy lives. We've also designed them to bring you closer together as a couple by showing you how to communicate about money in honest, respectful ways.

Before we launch into the Money Dump, however, we want to do a quick recap. Everything you've learned so far is going to come into play as you discover how to use these three tools. Your Money Personalities, the Opposite Dynamic, your partner's Money Personalities, and the causes of financial infidelity will all come into play as you unpack the issues you're dealing with as a couple and figure out what to do about them.

Take a minute to think about your Money Personalities, your spouse's Money Personalities, and the challenges and opportunities they create when they come together. Then think about those areas of financial infidelity you identified in the previous chapters. Consider how your Money Personalities have played into that financial infidelity.

Now you're ready for the Money Dump.

Getting It All Out

When I (Taylor) was growing up, my family always had an open-door policy for any kid who needed a hot meal or a place to stay. I remember one kid in particular who I didn't get along with. Most of the new faces fit in right away, but one boy and I just couldn't get on the same page. Finally, my mother got tired of it and came up with a plan for ironing things out. She had me and this other kid write down everything about each other that we found annoying. That part was pretty easy. I filled up the whole page in a few minutes. Then came the much tougher task—she made us write a list of things we liked about each other.

When we finished, I was expecting a long therapy session, but instead that was it. Mom thanked us for doing as she'd asked and let us get back to playing.

It seemed like a useless exercise for a few minutes, but then I quickly realized how much better I felt. Just taking the time to write that list of likes and dislikes released a ton of tension that had been building up. As far as I could tell, it had the same effect on the other boy. Dumping all those thoughts and feelings on a piece of paper was a cathartic task, even if nothing about our relationship expressly changed.

That's what the Money Dump is all about. It's a chance for you to dump out all the fears and worries and hopes you have for your Money Relationship. It's *not* the time to rip into your spouse or make a list of all their wrongdoings. You're not dumping *on* your spouse. You're dumping all the emotional crud inside you that's holding you back from really working *with* your spouse.

The Money Dump is also a way to celebrate the victories in your Money Relationship, no matter how insignificant they might seem. It's a way to name what's working so you can capitalize on your strengths. It's a way to show your spouse that you notice the contributions they make to the family. It's a way to talk about what's really happening in your Money Relationship.

Here's how it works.

The Money Dump

Step 1: Be Alone

Start in separate rooms. Get a piece of paper and a pencil and find a quiet spot to do your Money Dump. Being alone lets you get rid of any distractions so you can really focus, and it also helps you to be more honest. You aren't going to share everything on your list with your partner, so you have nothing to lose by being completely vulnerable with what you write. Find your own safe space and let the words fly.

Step 2: Pros and Cons

Make a line down the paper to divide it into two columns. On one side, write out all the pros of your Money Relationship: What are you grateful for? What gives you hope? What do you appreciate about your spouse? In the other column, list your cons. Remember, this isn't meant to become a list of all the ways your spouse has messed up your finances. It's a way to lay out all the stressors, the fears, and the challenges you see in your Money Relationship.

Here's what our friend Hannah's list looked like:

Pros: We have a house. We have jobs. We have a little money in savings. We are good at buying things on sale. We don't go out too much, so that saves money. Jerry is good

PROS

- ✓ We have a house.
- ✓ We have jobs.
- ✓ We have some money in our savings.
- ✓ We are good at buying things on sale.
- ✓ We don't go out often, so we save money.
- ✓ Jerry is good with money.
- ✓ We paid off student loans.
- ✓ We don't have much debt except our mortgage and car payment.

CONS

- ✓ We never do anything fun because it costs money.
- ✓ I feel like I can't spend money without Jerry's permission.
- ✓ I hate my job but can't afford to quit.
- ✓ Our mortgage is too high.
- ✓ We don't have enough saved for retirement, and time's running out.
- ✓ We haven't gone on vacation in five years.
- ✓ Jerry works too much overtime.
- ✓ We fight about money a lot.

with money. We paid off our student loans. We don't have much debt except our mortgage and a car payment. We can usually buy the kids the things they need for school. I'm a good bargain hunter. We know our Money Personalities: I'm a Saver/Security Seeker; Jerry is a Saver/Flyer. We don't have a lot of financial infidelity. We trust each other.

Cons: We never do anything fun because it costs too much. I feel like I can't spend money without Jerry's permission. I

PROS | CONS

PROS

- ☑ We can usually buy the kids items for school.

- ☑ I'm a good bargain hunter.

- ☑ We know both of our money personalities.

- ☑ We don't have a lot of financial infidelity.

- ☑ We trust each other.

CONS

- ☑ We have the Opposite Dynamic in our relationship.

- ☑ I want to help my parents out but we can't afford it.

- ☑ I get stressed during the holidays spending money on things they don't need.

hate my job but can't afford to quit. Our mortgage is too high. We don't have enough saved for retirement, and time's running out. We haven't gone on vacation in five years. Jerry works too much overtime. We fight about money a lot. We have the Opposite Dynamic. I want to help my parents out, but we can't afford it. I get stressed out during the holidays and birthdays because I hate spending money on gifts people don't need.

Step 3: Circle One Con

Choose the one con that's creating the most tension in your relationship. If there's an issue that's been bugging you and you just haven't known how to bring it up, this is your chance. You'll be sharing this con with your spouse, so make sure you find a way to talk about it that doesn't place all the blame on your spouse.

Hannah's con: We haven't gone on vacation in five years.

Step 4: Get Together

Sit down at the kitchen table or on the living room couch and look each other in the eyes. You are doing something *so* important for your relationship, and we want you to take a moment to look at each other and remember that you are in this together.

Step 5: Read Your List of Pros Out Loud

When we do the Money Dump with couples, we love watching this process unfold. There was one pair, Dan and Julie, who barely looked at each other when they arrived at the session. When we worked through the Money Dump with them, we weren't sure what to expect. They were having a hard time coming up with pros, so we suggested they start each item with the words "I appreciate that . . .". Julie started reading her list of pros and said, "I appreciate that you work so hard for our family." As soon as she said it, some of the tension was released from Dan's shoulders. You could see his defenses lowering.

Next it was his turn. He said, "I appreciate that you clip coupons."

She looked stunned. "I thought you hated that."

He looked just as surprised. "I never said that."

This time it was Julie's shoulders that softened. "Yeah, you're right. I guess you didn't."

They hadn't changed any behaviors yet, but they saw each other differently. They saw what was real in their Money Relationship—a sense of mutual respect and recognition. That simple conversation breathed life back into their relationship. For the rest of the session, they looked at each other, talked, and even laughed as though they were getting to know each other for the first time.

Step 6: Share Your One Con

One. Just one. Only one. Uno. We've found that in a lot of cases, both spouses have the same con. Even if you don't, you'll probably find that you have similar ideas about what you want to work on in your Money Relationship. Do your best during this step to stick with your own feelings about the situation you're discussing. Nothing good will come from blaming the other person. If you're concerned that your spouse is spending too much, explain why that concerns you: "I'm worried we won't have any money for retirement, and I really want to travel with you someday." Or, "I'd love to spend our money on things that really matter to us."

Step 7: Commit for Ninety Days

Commit to working on each of your cons for the next ninety days. These two cons might not get solved, but you'll be working on them together. Over the next two chapters, we'll explain the Money Huddle—a regular time to get together and work out a plan for dealing with the other cons. For now, just figure out what you want to work on. That's it. It might not seem like much, but think about it like this: until you started reading this book, you weren't doing anything to improve your Money Relationship. If this is the only thing you do after reading this book, you'll have improved your relationship by leaps and bounds.

We suggest doing the Money Dump once a year. That's

it. Just once a year. In between, keep track of your cons and celebrate your progress, even when it's just a little step in the right direction. Keep thinking up pros and cons to add to next year's list. You'll be surprised how quickly the list grows.

In the next two chapters, we're going to show you how to use the Money Huddle to keep the momentum going.

PROS | CONS

Make It Happen

OKAY, go ahead and do your Money
Dump. No, really. You're ready. Good luck!

(For more Money Dump resources,
go to TheMoneyCouple.com.)

TEN

The Money Huddle

THE Money Dump is a turning point for a lot of couples. For many of them it's the first time they've gotten all these feelings about their Money Relationship out. It's usually the first time they've taken an honest look at what's working, which can feel really good.

There's something refreshing about getting all that crud out of your system, but if you stop there, you're missing out on the best part of rebuilding your Money Relationship, which is what happens during the Money Huddle.

The Money Huddle is a time you and your spouse set aside to talk about your Money Relationship. In the next chapter we'll give you an easy outline to guide you through your Money Huddle. Before we do that, we want to help you understand what this little sit-down is really about.

Being Intentional

The vast majority of couples we meet are consumed by worry. They are worried about their debt. They are worried about their savings. They are worried about their future. This excessive worry is a big reason why their Money Relationships are a mess. They're so stressed out that even those little decisions like where to eat dinner or what kind of coffee to buy turn into major fights.

They think all that worry and stress are about their budget, but we all know that's not true. The problem is deeply rooted in their Money Relationship. No matter how much debt you're in or how little money you have saved up, it's possible to have a strong, healthy Money Relationship, but only if you know how to separate the details of your finances from the details of your personal partnership.

By now you've read enough that you know the difference between your finances and your Money Relationship. Remember Jonell and Kai? We told you all about their income and expenses and debt in chapter 2. That was their financial situation. It was *not* their Money Relationship. Just as we had Jonell and Kai do, we're now asking you to be intentional about separating your financial situation from your Money Relationship. The best way to do this effectively is by using the Money Huddle.

The Money Huddle is not the time to balance your checkbook or pay your bills. It's not the time to gripe at your husband about how much he spent getting the car detailed or to blame your wife for not keeping all of her receipts organized. It's not the time to look over your retirement plans or talk through potential investments. In other words, the Money Huddle is not the time to deal with your financial situation.

Instead, this is the time to reconnect, to build trust, to work together on assessing the present and dreaming about the future.

It would be great if conversations like this just happened spontaneously. For the most part, most of us just don't have time to focus on the emotional side of our Money Relationship. Without that time and connection, we lose our patience and yell or blame or get irritated and stew. That's how money starts to throw a marriage off track.

You've done a lot of hard work to get this far. Now it's time to take advantage of your well-earned progress and keep moving forward. When you set aside time each month to talk through the realities of your financial situation, to tell your spouse how you can be supported, to ask your spouse how you can best support them, and to dream about the future together, you can put an end to fights, stop blaming each other, and grow closer than you've been in a long time.

The Money Huddle Defined

When we talk with couples about the Money Huddle, they assume it's a time to do their family bookkeeping together. That's actually the last thing we want you to do. At the risk of sounding repetitive, we're going to run through this one more time. There's a practical side to your Money Relationship—managing your money, balancing the books, paying the bills. For many couples, that's where the understanding of their Money Relationship stops. They don't realize that this connection is really about the emotional repercussions of all their money decisions. Your budget and your Money Relationship are not the same thing. Our goal with the Money Huddle is to pull the practical and emotional sides apart. This clarifies the distinction and helps you really focus on the emotional baggage that comes with the daily onslaught of financial decisions and related stressors.

There are four reasons why we want you to keep the practical side and emotional side of your Money Relationship separate.

1. *The separation keeps the Money Huddle from feeling like a meeting.* In most relationships there is a "money person," the one who sets the budget and pays the bills. If your Money Huddle is all about the practical side of your Money Relationship, it's a fairly one-sided affair. It just isn't feasible or enjoyable for most couples to pay their bills together, so one person takes on that responsibility. Your Money Huddle will be a major failure if it boils down to one person holding a meeting while the other one just listens. Instead, this is a time for compromise, mutual respect, and joint decision-making. It's a time to look ahead together.

2. *It defuses the tension.* Most of us get a little anxious when we're paying bills and looking over our accounts. It's not the best time to bring up plans or needs or ideas about how you can strengthen your communication. Having a separate Money Huddle

gives you a little emotional distance from the imme-
diate demands of your finances.

3. *It puts the focus on your relationship.* If the only time
you talk about your Money Relationship is when
you're putting a mortgage payment in the mail, it's
easy to think that your budget is the defining factor in your relationship. Not the case. What matters
are your Money Personalities, the impact of your
Opposite Dynamics, and the financial infidelity that
threatens to pull you and your spouse apart. Having
a Money Huddle gives you the time and mental space
you need to deal with those issues.

4. *It keeps you close and connected.* It might be hard to
imagine right now, but we promise that if you stay
committed to a monthly Money Huddle and use that
time to talk through your Money Relationship, you
will reclaim the intimacy you once had and want in
your marriage. You will find ways to keep money
from being a source of anguish and instead allow
your Money Relationship to draw you together in
ways you've only dreamed about.

Not long ago, we had a couple come in for a meeting.
They arrived in separate cars and hardly looked at each
other while we talked with them. We asked them to commit
to a Money Dump and at least one Money Huddle. They
agreed and left the office looking as miserable as they had
when they'd first arrived.

A month later they came back. They held hands while
they sat in the reception area. They laughed together when

they told us how they'd stumbled through their first Money Huddle. They finished each other's sentences as they told us about the dreams they came up with while they talked. They walked out of the office smiling at each other and exchanged a kiss or two before getting in the car together and heading home. You might have a slightly longer road to smooching it up in front of your financial planner, but we're confident that if you commit to these regular, focused, honest times of conversation, you're going to grow closer.

We know that for a lot of couples the idea of adding one more commitment to an already overloaded life feels like too much to ask. We've kept the Money Huddle simple to make it easier for you to find the time. It's forty-five minutes, once a month. In the next chapter we'll lay out exactly how you'll use that forty-five minutes. If you think of this as an investment in your relationship, a chance to reclaim the life you used to dream about, then that seems like a pretty reasonable price to pay.

Make It Happen

TAKE some time to discuss what you are looking forward to and what fears you have about doing the Money Huddle together.

ELEVEN

Begin with the E.N.D.

IN his bestselling book *The 7 Habits of Highly Effective People,* Stephen Covey suggests that those who want to be successful in life should "begin with the end in mind." That's certainly true when it comes to your Money Relationship. You need to have a vision for what a successful marriage could look like. We find that most couples have a fairly simple vision. They want to stop fighting. They want a relationship in which they work together instead of battling against each other. They want to make decisions without arguing and solve problems without blaming.

It's important to ask yourself: What do you want?

Think about that question for a minute. What do you want your Money Relationship to be like? Do you want to be equal partners in making financial decisions, or are you okay with having a "money person"? Can you accept the occasional argument as long as it doesn't get nasty and personal? Are you willing to cut back on spending or reduce your savings in order to have a more peaceful Money Relationship? If you come to your first Money Huddle with a clear vision for the future, you're going to have a much easier time listening to each other and accepting compromise than if you just show up and expect your problems to take care of themselves.

This is where your Money Dump will come in handy. Remember the cons you identified? They can be your guide to creating a vision for your Money Relationship.

In the previous chapter, Hannah's con was that she and her husband, Jerry, hadn't gone on vacation in five years. That's a big con. For Hannah a healthy Money Relationship is one that balances security and savings with regular doses of fun, rest, and exciting experiences together. That's a clear, doable goal, one Jerry can sign on to as well.

Once you have a vision for your Money Relationship, you have to be intentional about making that vision a reality. You have to be committed to developing new patterns of communication. You have to be willing to give up some longstanding habits. You have to be willing to set aside forty-five minutes a month to talk about your Money Relationship.

The E.N.D.

We use the acronym E.N.D. to help you keep your Money Huddle focused. The fastest way to kill the momentum you have right now is to turn your Money Huddle into a two-hour gripefest or let it devolve into a conversation about the details of your IRA. Instead, keep your time short and to the point, and pull out your phone's timer to keep you on track if you have to. Your forty-five minutes will be broken into three fifteen-minute chunks, each of them focused on one task.

Evaluate

Use the first fifteen minutes of your Money Huddle to evaluate your current financial situation. We know, we just said this wasn't the time to talk about your financial situation. Still, we want you to deal with the real story of your financial life as you work on your Money Relationship. Keep your conversation limited to the two biggest issues in your finances—debt and savings. We can't stress how important it is to stick with these two topics and nothing else. These are the areas that create the most tension in a relationship; most of us have too much of one and not enough of the other. You're not going to discuss every expense or deposit—you can do that later. You're just getting a general overview of where you are right now. There should be two numbers to review, one for debt and one for savings. If you see a third number, that's one too many.

This step is simple, but it's the key to putting an end to financial infidelity. Financial infidelity thrives on secrets. It feeds off a spouse's acceptance to remain in the dark about the realities of a couple's money. A quick evaluation shines a light on what's real. When you know the truth about your financial picture, you can start making plans and moving forward. You can finally get rid of the fear, anxiety, and mistrust, and truly start over.

This is where the money person in the relationship gets to report on what's happening with the family's savings and debt. That doesn't mean the money person gets to dominate the conversation. Their job is to lay out the facts then spend the rest of the fifteen minutes working on a mutual plan for how to reduce debt and increase savings.

Start with the money you have put away—all of it. What do you have in your retirement account? The kids' college fund? How about emergency funds, vacation funds, a house-buying fund? Lay it all on the table and talk about where you are versus where you want to be. What kind of realistic changes can you make that will move you closer to your goals? If you're not sure where to start, we have all kinds of planning tools on our website, TheMoneyCouple.com, to get you going.

After savings, move on to debt. Look at your car payments, your mortgage, any loans you have, any personal debt you owe. As you do, remember that your debt isn't the issue. You can get out of debt, no matter how impossible it may seem. What's really important is that you communicate, that you work together to come up with solutions, and that you move forward instead of looking back.

One more word about debt. We know a lot of financial advisors who put the fear of God into people about debt. They treat it as though it's the child of the devil himself. While debt can obviously be devastating, it is not the real problem for most couples.

As I (Taylor) divulged in the intro, I've been deep in debt—plenty of thousands of dollars which I did not have the means to pay back. By the time I understood how much I owed and what the interest was doing to me—things Megan had realized immediately—I was terrified and full of regret.

Fortunately, it didn't tear our relationship apart. If anything, Megan's helping me map out a repayment plan brought us closer together. She could have pointed out the mistakes I'd made while taking zero responsibility herself, but instead she chose to work with me, allowing us to conquer together the problem I'd created. That unified front helped us clean up our financial picture and made us more optimistic about what we could accomplish in the future—together.

Unfortunately, we know couples who have called it quits over far less debt than I had to deal with. It's a sad thing to see, especially because the debt clearly wasn't the issue. If they'd ignored the credit cards for a few weeks and focused on their Money Relationship, those marriages could have survived.

If you have debt, don't beat yourself up over it. It's just how life works sometimes, and there's nothing to be gained by feeling ashamed or guilty about owing money. Those feelings can quickly spiral into inaction, blame, and more financial infidelity. Stop listening to the voices that tell you debt is from the devil. It's not. It's just debt.

Whether you are $5,000 or $50,000 in the hole, we want you to face the realities of your financial situation together. We want you to figure out how to deal with that situation as a couple. We want you to see yourself as true partners and move forward hand in hand.

The *Evaluate* part of your Money Huddle might be a little painful the first time you work through it. If you've had years of financial infidelity in your Money Relationship, you'll have all kinds of secrets to untangle. Keep in mind that you don't have to deal with all of it at once. Take it one

Money Huddle at a time, and you can get through this. Do everything in your power to resist blaming each other and instead focus on how you can fix it. You're making a fresh start, and this process is only going to get easier.

Needs

The next fifteen minutes of your Money Huddle is the time to talk about what you need in your Money Relationship. Most of us are terrible at telling other people what we need, especially when it comes to money. We assume our spouses know that we have a hunting weekend planned for the same weekend every year or that we need a new outfit for a big presentation at work. They might know this information in general, but focused communication always makes things clearer.

This is the time to keep everything you've learned about your Money Personalities in the forefront. If your spouse is a Security Seeker and he tells you he needs the family to cut back on spending, you know it's not because he's trying to be controlling; it's because he's worried. Talk about this anxiety. Ask what he needs in order to feel secure. If you're a Spender and you're feeling the pinch of a tighter budget, talk about your need to have some freedom in your spending. Ask about setting up a small discretionary fund that gives you some leeway without busting the budget.

This is also the time to look at the cons you chose during your Money Dump. Those cons are really *needs* in disguise. Talk about what you need to get that con off your list. If it's a vacation, just say so and start planning. If it's more trust, just say so and start breaking down the walls that have built up.

By being honest about your needs, you show your spouse that you trust them, that you value their insight, and that you believe the two of you can work together to solve problems. That kind of affirmation goes a long way toward connecting you as a couple.

Dream

The final fifteen-minute segment of the Money Huddle is our favorite. This is when you're going to spark your dreams again and put together a plan for making them happen. It's a monthly deposit in your Money Relationship that will add up quickly.

We see it over and over again. When couples dream together, they move forward together. Conversely, when they stop dreaming, their relationship stops growing. Take this time each month to envision the future you want to build with your spouse by your side.

During one of our Money Huddles, we started talking about our retirement. We love to travel, but we aren't sure if that's all we'll want to do in our later years. So we came up with a very tentative plan: we'll see where our kids are living at that point and spend time settling down near them. We might not have to go anywhere, or we might have to leave the country for a stretch, and the uncertainty is actually kind of exciting.

It's not exactly a plan—more of a working theory—but it suits us, our family, and the comfort we want to enjoy down the road. Now that we have this idea, we can be a little more purposeful as we put money into our retirement. That dream, while far off on the horizon, helps motivate us to continue saving. Since we share the same dream, we get to work together to *Make It Happen.*

This is the time to talk about short-term dreams and long-term dreams, personal dreams, and dreams for your family. Nothing is off-limits. Maybe you want to take a pottery class. Now is the time to bring that up and talk about your schedule. Maybe you want to help your aging parents with their healthcare costs. Maybe you want to stay home with your kids or start a new job or move into a different house. Most of these dreams existed early in your relationship, and now you have a chance to get them back.

Whatever your dreams are, talk about them and start planning for them. We suggest couples bring a calendar to their Money Huddles. The process of dreaming together will draw you closer and build a deeper sense of connection and intimacy.

The Money Huddle brings together all the skills and knowledge you've developed while reading this book. As the months go by and you stay committed to monthly Money Huddles, you'll see your Money Relationship change dramatically. You'll put an end to constant battles, mistrust, resentment, and financial infidelity, and you'll replace them with meaningful conversations about your life together. That's worth more than any bank account.

Something else happens when you use this time to talk about what you need from your Money Relationship. You'll actually stop talking about money all the time. When you know you have time set aside to deal with issues that come up during the month, you'll find that you don't talk about them over every meal or as you're getting ready for bed.

When you free yourself from the constant stress of talking about finances, you suddenly have time to talk about other, more important things.

Take one couple we worked with recently. He was a Flyer/Spender; she was a Security Seeker/Saver. You know enough about Money Personalities now to recognize that this relationship could have been a disaster. It wasn't a disaster when we met with them, but there were signs it might be headed that way. He spent money they didn't have; she was freaking out about it.

We encouraged them to try holding regular Money Huddles and report back to us in a couple of months. Sure enough, they came back with a renewed commitment to make their marriage work. The Money Huddles, they said, had been a great tool for helping them manage the way they talked about money. For a long time he'd been frustrated that all of their conversations seemed to eventually come back to his spending. She was frustrated that he didn't seem to listen to her requests that he spend less.

By implementing the monthly Money Huddle, they created a forum for talking about these issues in a calm way rather than in the heat of a disagreement. When their daily conversations started to turn into money conversations, he could ask her to table that concern and bring it up in their next Money Huddle. When she did as he requested, he ended up being much more receptive to listening to her concerns and figuring out compromises in his spending habits. She felt heard, he felt that the nagging had stopped, and they could both see that their Money Relationship was on the mend.

Make It Happen

PLAN your first Money Huddle. Do it, right now. Go get your spouse and your calendar and find forty-five minutes to start your new Money Relationship with the E.N.D. in mind.

PART 3

RECLAIMING YOUR MARRIAGE

TWELVE

Why We Fight

IT might seem strange to talk about fighting when we've just taken you through the Money Huddle lovefest. Here's the thing: no matter how great you get at communicating, no matter how well you understand each other's Money Personalities, no matter how many dreams you work toward, you're still going to fight about money.

The tools we've given you aren't magic. They aren't going to make you suddenly agree on every money decision. And although they will dramatically reduce the number of arguments you have about finances, they won't prevent you from ever having a heated conversation about saving and spending. We know because we still have those fights ourselves.

In the next chapter we'll show you how to keep those fights from escalating into hurtful arguments that leave permanent emotional scars. Before we touch on that, we want to show you why fights about money can be so painful and damaging to a relationship.

Hitting the Core

We had a couple in our office who had been married for about five years. He'd grown up with a lot of money, and she'd grown up with very little. He was a Saver, she was a Spender, and the Opposite Dynamic was a major factor in their relationship. Their situation was a lot like mine (Megan's) and Taylor's, and we immediately noticed that they were dealing with a lot of the same baggage we had worked through.

That's why it didn't surprise me when their conversation turned into a shouting match. I could tell this was an old fight, one they had come back to over and over, and I remembered the times when Taylor and I had to deal with this conflict multiple times each week.

The fundamental issue between them was that she was spending more than he thought she should. They fought about what she spent and where she spent it. After listening for a few minutes, we stopped them. "Hang on," we said. "Let's get to the heart of this problem. Why do you keep spending when he's asking you not to? Why won't you stick to the budget?"

She had a strong answer ready to go. "My parents were missionaries, and I grew up dirt-poor. We had two meals a day if we were lucky. We didn't always have toilet paper. Now my husband makes a great living, and I don't see why he won't let me spend money. I deserve to have nice things after spending so much of my life with nothing."

He looked at her like he'd never heard this before.

We turned to him, giving him a chance to respond. "I don't trust you with our money," he said. "I'm afraid you're going to bankrupt us, and we won't have a future if you keep spending like this."

Her jaw just hit the ground.

They both realized that the other person had deep-seated needs that weren't being met in their Money Relationship, needs that were part of their very different Money Personalities. Those differences had led to intense arguments that had left both of them emotionally bruised.

Arguments about money hurt us like very few other fights do. They feel intensely personal. We feel attacked and get defensive. We walk away from them filled with anger, resentment, and a deep sense of mistrust. For a long time we didn't understand why money fights seemed to create such complex, long-term problems for couples. When we finally thought about how deeply embedded our Money Personalities are, it all started to make sense.

So often money fights are the result of our different perspectives on money. We look at the way the other person makes decisions, and we just don't get it. Our response is to criticize and attack these differences, and that's why money fights hurt so much. Our Money Personalities are so deeply personal, so central to who we are, that to insult them is to insult us at our core. It doesn't feel as if your spouse is criticizing your actions; it feels as if they are criticizing who you are.

In truth, that's exactly what's happening. Your Money Personalities are as much a part of you as your eye color or the size of your feet. You have as much a chance of changing it as you do of making your feet two sizes bigger.

Most of us are fairly aware of our flaws. You know if you have a tendency to be impatient or irritable or a procrastinator. While we don't like hearing other people name our faults, we know they're right when they do. With our Money Personalities, we really don't see our way of thinking as flawed. Each of us believes our method is the right way to approach financial decisions. When someone we love tells us our method is stupid, irrational, or crazy, it feels very different from someone pointing out a standard personality flaw. It feels as if they are attacking the good parts of who we are, not the parts we recognize as needing work. When we believe we've been acting in the best interests of our families, it hurts even more to hear our spouse rattle off the ways we're failing them.

Cal is a Saver's Saver. His friends tell him he's cheap, and he laughs it off because he knows it's true. He prides himself on getting a lot for a little, on living off next to nothing, and on making his way without help from anyone. He paid his way through college by working three jobs and living for free with a couple he met through his church. Sure, he slept on a cot in their unfinished basement, but he didn't care. Free was free. He could feed himself for a week on one of those rotisserie chickens from the grocery store. His entire wardrobe was made up of stuff from the thrift store and castoffs from the older son of the couple he lived with.

Believe it or not, Cal found a woman who didn't mind his Saver ways. Carmen thought Cal was charming, and she loved how nonmaterialistic and free-spirited he seemed to be. He would make her funky little gifts out of old magazines or cereal boxes, and she thought they were the coolest trinkets she'd ever seen.

Unsurprisingly, Cal's thrifty ways started to lose their

charm after a few years of marriage. Cal was a social studies teacher at the middle school in town, and Carmen was a nurse. Together they made a reasonable living, enough to afford a little house and two used cars. They eventually had a couple of children and a lovely life together.

Through it all, Cal never let go of his fervent frugality. Even when they could afford to do otherwise, he insisted they wash out their plastic bags and reuse aluminum foil. He wore his socks until they had holes in the heels and the toes and refused to let Carmen buy him new pants, even when his trusty khakis were worn almost bare in the knees.

Most frustrating for Carmen was Cal's unwillingness to buy her something nice for her birthday, their anniversary, Christmas, or any other occasion. She still loved the sweet homemade cards he gave her, but part of her really wanted some killer earrings, just once. She had come right out and told him so on more than one occasion, but it didn't seem to take. For Carmen, Cal's refusal to spend money on her felt like he was more concerned with saving money than he was with her feelings.

On her most recent birthday, Carmen reached the limits of her patience. She opened her card and asked if Cal had gotten her a gift. Before he could answer, she looked at him and said sarcastically, "Wait, let me guess. You made me a diamond necklace out of tinfoil and a paper clip. Gee, I'm so glad you didn't have to spend any money on me."

Cal was stunned. She'd always liked his little home-made cards and gifts. Why was she suddenly so angry? He asked her directly, and that's when it all came out. Years and years of feeling slighted by her husband's thrifty ways came

pouring out of Carmen. She told him he was stingy, cheap, and selfish. Cal was crushed.

From his perspective it was his willingness to do without that had helped him get where he was. He drove an old car and saved every penny he could so they could afford a nice house. He never asked for Christmas gifts because he wanted to make sure they could afford something nice for their kids. He never bought new clothes because he wanted to make sure they'd be able to send the kids to college. In his mind it was his cheapness that allowed them to live so well. Carmen's words hit Cal right in the gut. As a result, it would take a lot of work to repair the relational damage that exchange had created.

If you and your spouse want to prevent money arguments from reaching that hurtful level, you have to respect each other's Money Personalities and avoid making them the center of your conflicts.

Behind the Conflict

Our Money Personalities aren't the cause of money fights, but unless we have an awareness of how others perceive our outlook on finances, we can fall into some bad habits that can lead to terrible friction.

In our years of working with couples, we've seen three main causes behind money fights.

We Don't Own Our Money Personalities

Your Money Personalities can be awesome. It can lead you to great wealth; it can keep you from ending up deep in debt; it can help you provide for your family; it can inspire you to acts of tremendous generosity. Nevertheless, it also comes with some baggage, which we ignore at our own risk.

So many of the arguments we see are the result of one or both spouses ignoring the downside of their Money Personalities. We know Spenders who refuse to acknowledge their impulsivity. We know Savers who are downright stingy and proud of it. That failure to own up to the challenges of their Money Personalities makes these people incredibly hard to work with, let alone live with.

If you really want to stop arguing about money all the time, you have to be willing to accept your Money Personalities—the good and the not-so-good. You have to be humble enough to see where you've contributed to the broken Money Relationship and strong enough to change your ways, or at least admit that change is needed.

We Act Out of Selfishness

Almost all of the financial infidelity we see is the result of (at least) one spouse's selfishness. When they get caught, they have nothing but excuses:

- "I was afraid we were going to lose all our money on your business deal, so I kept some cash for myself."
- "I wanted to be able to shop whenever I wanted, so I opened my own credit card."
- "I really wanted that new car, so I tapped into our kids' college account."
- "I like to go out to eat, so if you don't want to go with me, I'll go out with friends instead."

Anytime we keep the focus on ourselves and what we want, no matter what it costs us in relationship capital, we're asking for a fight. It's hard to blame someone for getting angry when their spouse has acted in a way that completely disregards the other person.

If you have a history of financial infidelity in your Money Relationship, this is the time to end it for good. It won't be easy. You'll have to keep reminding yourself not to make false assumptions about your spouse. You'll have to risk trusting them even if you've been burned before. You'll have to be willing to give up what you want for the sake of your relationship. No one can make the effort on your behalf; you have to do the work.

We Get Money Grumpy

Our Money Personalities give us a kind of personal comfort zone. Spenders like being in stores with total purchasing power. Put a Spender on a tight budget and they're going to get grumpy. Meanwhile you take a Saver on a superfluous shopping spree and they're going to be in a sour mood.

It might sound silly to talk about a grumpy Saver, but when Savers are pushed out of their comfort zones, they can act like animals who have been torn from their natural habitat. Savers get aggressive, defensive, and protective, and that leads to some nasty arguments.

You probably have plenty of stories of your own to prove this point. Nearly every money conflict has some element of the money grumps in it. You come home from the store, and your Security Seeker spouse wants to see your receipt. You get defensive, they're already anxious, and before you know it—BAM! A simple shopping trip has sparked a shouting match.

You can't avoid getting money grumpy. Sooner or later, you're going to be forced out of your Money Personality comfort zone. The thing you can control is how you react to the perceived threat. Instead of getting defensive, anxious, or protective, figure out how to be yourself in that situation. If you're a Spender with a budget, challenge yourself to do more with less. If you're a Saver tagging along on a shopping spree, see what kind of deals you can find. Get comfortable in your own skin, and you'll find you don't need to indulge that negative reaction. You can take whatever comes and make it work for you.

You've done great work so far. Even with all the new information and tools we've loaded on you, you're still two people with two different perspectives on money. No matter how hard you work, there will still be decisions made that your partner doesn't understand and vice versa. However, when you feel close to your spouse, when you remember that you have shared goals and dreams for your shared future, you won't want to hurt each other. If you do cause your spouse emotional pain, you will want to make it right. That's what happens when your Money Relationship is working.

Make It Happen

IT'S hard to stop fighting when all you can see is the negative side of your spouse. Try to change your view for a minute. Make an appreciation list for your spouse. Write down three or four aspects of your spouse's Primary Money Personality that are making a positive difference in your Money Relationship. When you're done, share your list.

THIRTEEN

How to Fight Fair

I have a client who is a professional athlete. A couple years back, he signed with a new team in a different part of the country. While he was meeting with new personnel and signing his contract, he decided to do a little house hunting. By the end of the day, not only had he found a great house for his family, he'd bought it!

He called his wife from the hotel later that night to tell her the good news. Contrary to what he'd expected, his wife was livid.

If you're a Spender, a Risk Taker, or a Flyer, you might wonder why she got so upset. He had nothing but good intentions and was doing what he thought was best for his family.

If you're a Saver or a Security Seeker, however, you probably got nervous just reading that story. The idea of your spouse spending that kind of money without your input feels like the worst kind of betrayal.

It took years for my client and his wife to recover from

this incident. She didn't trust him; he felt like she didn't respect him. It was a long, ugly fight that ran like a current under their relationship for a long, long time.

No matter what your Money Personalities are, no matter what your past looks like, no matter how committed you are to building a better future, you are going to have disagreements about money. What you do with those disagreements is what will separate your successful marriage from the average, money-troubled relationship.

The Rules of Engagement

Remember those fire safety demonstrations you saw in elementary school? The firefighters would visit the school to talk about smoke detectors and escape routes and all those other ways of staying safe in case of fire. The one that usually sticks with everyone best is what you're supposed to do if you're on fire: Stop, Drop, and Roll!

Stop, Drop, and Roll is good advice for putting out emotional fires too. Here's how it works.

Stop

Let's say your husband comes home from running errands one Saturday and pulls a nice new pair of skis out of the back of the van. The old you might have stood in the doorway with that look of disapproval clouding your face, just daring him to bring them in the house. When he did, that's when the sparks would fly. "What on earth did you do? We can't afford those! What were you thinking?" In a few short minutes, you're in the thick of a vicious argument.

What if you stopped yourself? What if you didn't say anything about the skis in the heat of the money moment and let yourself settle down for a bit first? Instead of yelling at your husband or accusing him of being an idiot, imagine what would happen if you just told him how you felt. You might say in a calm and measured way, "Honey, I thought we'd agreed we would talk about any purchases over fifty dollars. Can you help me understand why you bought these skis without talking to me about it?"

Not only is the whole tone of that statement less accusatory, but it also leaves room for your spouse to either offer a good explanation or admit his mistake and find a way to make it right. Maybe they were on clearance, maybe he bought them as a gift, or maybe he'll end up returning them the next day. At least he has the opportunity to state his claim and then make a thoughtful decision.

The simple act of stopping yourself from reacting out of anger can defuse a potentially explosive argument before it starts. That doesn't mean you never speak up; you have every right to advocate for your needs. But when you take a breath and simmer down before reacting, you can talk about your feelings instead of making it all about the money. Reminder: it's not about the money.

Drop

They say that assumptions are the lowest form of knowledge. That's certainly true in a Money Relationship.

That's why the second rule to remember is to drop your assumptions.

The vast majority of money fights start with an overblown preconception. You assume your spouse was dishonest when she failed to mention the $40 she spent on lunch with friends, when the truth is that she's a Flyer who didn't think it was worth mentioning. You assume your spouse is being controlling about your spending when in reality she's been trying to limit extraneous expenses because she's planning a family vacation.

A year ago, Megan came home to find an email from an RV dealership in Dallas. The subject of the email had a line like "Welcome to life with an RV!" or some such thing. We had discussed the idea of buying a home we could take on the road, but the conversation was mostly me dreaming of an adventure and Megan reminding me those adventures aren't always as picturesque as social media makes them out to be. When Megan came home to find an enthusiastic message about my plans to buy an RV, she quickly assumed I (Taylor) had gone ahead and spent $200,000 on a thing only one of us wanted. Like any Saver married to an impulsive Spender, to say she was upset would be an understatement.

I didn't hear about this right away. It wasn't until later that Megan told me she'd had her phone out, ready to call me at work and chew my ear off for making such a huge decision without her. Obviously, that call didn't happen. She instead decided to sit tight, take a deep breath, and wait for me to come home so we could talk in person.

By the time I got home, Megan had reread the email and realized it wasn't a bill but an estimate—one I had requested, even though I knew my RV dreams were not about to come true. She asked me about it, and I described the aggressive sales pitch coming from the person on the phone and how I'd asked for the prices just to end the conversation.

The talk lasted about four minutes. Did we decide to buy an RV? Sadly, no. Did we go to sleep angry? Quite the opposite.

Dropping your assumptions allows you to see what's real in a situation. When you see that reality, you can deal with it much more gracefully. You can ask questions, talk about what went wrong, and find a solution. You can't do any of that when you're too busy assuming what happened.

Roll

The final rule for fighting fair is to roll up your sleeves and find a way to work together. When it comes to resolving money conflicts, there is no substitute for compromise and cooperation. One story that comes to mind happened right after our good friends Josh and Allison got married and he wanted to buy the latest gaming console. Their agreed-upon price was around $250. However, when he came home, he had a car full of games, headsets, adaptors, and a console that cost $500. He had doubled the price of the thing he was supposed to be buying, then added another $300 of games and gadgets on top of that—from $250 to $800, just like that. The look on Allison's face told him all he needed to know about his decision.

While Josh isn't the type to suffer from buyer's remorse very often, he can recognize the times he *should* feel buyer's remorse. Before Allison could explain why she thought he'd done the wrong thing, he'd already pulled out the receipt to confirm he could return it all. After Josh took everything back and got the money refunded, they talked about how they might find compromise in this and future similar situations. Yes, they ended up back at square one, but the good news is that it felt like a joint decision.

A lot of couples we work with have forgotten how to compromise. Once you've learned about each other's Money Personalities, once you've started expressing your needs in your Money Huddles, once you've begun the repair work on your Money Relationship, it becomes a whole lot easier to find a path forward that meets everyone's needs.

You're going to have conflicts about money. One day, maybe even tomorrow, one of you will make a decision that drives the other crazy. That person could blow up and have a fit, or they could *stop* and take some time to cool down, *drop* the assumptions and look for what's real, and *roll* up their sleeves to start the work of solving the problem. That's how a potential problem turns into an opportunity to strengthen your Money Relationship.

Make It Happen

TAKE time for each of you to share a story where you could have used Stop, Drop, and Roll to resolve a situation.

CONCLUSION

YOU should be very proud of yourselves. You've done something amazing, something that will change your marriage for good. We know this stuff isn't always easy—sometimes it can be downright painful. We also know that when couples commit to changing their patterns, when they join hands and move forward together, they can accomplish anything.

You might wrap up this book and still be deep in debt. You probably haven't made a big deposit in your retirement account while reading it. Your financial picture might not be any better than it was when you opened up chapter 1. But you know what? That's okay. You have made significant deposits in your relationship. You have taken momentous steps toward building a strong, healthy, thriving Money Relationship. That's so much more important than any budget or savings plan.

You've learned about your Money Personalities and come to understand that each of us has our own way of thinking about and dealing with money. You've discovered that the Opposite Dynamic can create a sense of internal conflict when it comes to your personal money decisions, but you've also seen how your Opposite Dynamic can help you stay balanced and make smart money choices.

You've learned about your spouse's Money Personality and how it connects and collides with yours. You've seen that when you play off each other's strengths, you can conquer any money problem that comes up.

If you've had a history of financial infidelity in your marriage, we hope it's been brought to light and kicked to the curb. Of everything we've covered in this book, this might be the one thing that takes the longest to unpack, especially if you have years of secrets and hiding and lies to deal with. You don't have to fix everything today, and you probably couldn't if you tried. You have time, and now you have a renewed sense of trust. We know that if you're both committed to transparency in all of your money decisions, it won't take long to repair the damage caused by financial infidelity.

You also have tools to take all of this knowledge and turn it into real action. Use your Money Dump to get everything out in the open, and then stick with your Money Huddles to keep the momentum going and plan your way back to your dreams.

When you find yourselves arguing about money, remember to Stop, Drop, and Roll to put out the flames of conflict and get yourselves cooled off. We know there will be times when you slip back into old patterns, but slipping doesn't mean you have to get stuck there. Stand up and try again. Soon the new habits will become your new lifestyle.

Every marriage begins with a million dreams. Each decision you make together will take you one step closer to reclaiming those dreams and returning to that same joyful couple you were on your wedding day.

In closing, we encourage you to pray this prayer together as a step of mutual surrender and humility:

Dear Lord, we thank you for our marriage. As we work together to strengthen our relationship, we ask that You be at the center of everything we do. From the words we speak to one another, to the action-able ways we show our love, thank you for giving us your wisdom and for teaching us to give each other grace—just as you so freely gave. Remind us that we should be slow to speak and quick to listen. Help us as we navigate our financial journey together to be good stewards of everything you have provided for us. Thank you for your peace that surpasses all understanding; may that peace reside in our home and lives as we continue to make our marriage a priority. We ask all of these things in Jesus' name, amen.

APPENDIX

The Five Money Personalities
Survival Guide

YOU know that in one way or another, money has an impact on every decision you make. That's why our Money Personalities play such an important role in our relationships. There are a handful of big moments that get our Money Personalities pumping harder than others—namely birthdays, holidays, and vacations. These are the times our Money Personalities go into overdrive, which can make an already stressful situation even worse.

When you know about these triggers and understand your partner's Money Personalities, you can anticipate the stress points and work together to defuse a potential problem before it turns into an argument. You can see past the short temper or the anxiety or the efforts to control the situation and get to the heart of what's happening inside your spouse.

Here's what to expect from each of the five Money

Personalities during some of the most stressful money moments in life. For a more extensive survival guide, head to TheMoneyCouple.com.

The Saver

We live in a culture of spending, and that's never as evident as it is during these money moments. That means the Saver is constantly surrounded by pressure to buy more, spend more, and give more. Take it from me (Megan)—that's very stressful. The Saver will respond to this pressure by trying to control their spending and the spending of everyone in their family.

Here's how to help your Saver conquer the mountain of stress that comes from the big money moments:

Holidays. During the holidays, the Saver will complain about every purchase that comes into the house—the gifts, the food, the wrapping paper. They'll get downright Grinchy about the whole thing, and that adds to everyone's stress. The nice thing about holidays is that you can plan for them. That's exactly what the Saver needs to do in order to have a Merry Christmas.

Well before a holiday arrives, sit down with your Saver and talk through your budget for the big day, getting as detailed as you can. Think about gifts, travel, and extra food for parties or visiting family. Then make a plan for setting aside the money you'll need before anyone spends a nickel. When a Saver knows there's money in the bank to cover holiday expenses, they can relax and enjoy the festivities.

Birthdays. Like other holidays, birthdays can bring out the worst in a Saver. Once again, planning ahead is a huge help. You can also help your Saver manage the spending stress of birthdays by setting up clear expectations. Most Savers feel a lot better about a purchase when they know they're spending their money on something useful, something they know the recipient will enjoy. Buying something for the sake of buying it feels like a waste of money for a Saver.

If your birthday is coming up, give your Saver spouse a few ideas for gifts you'd like. That gives them some options on price point but also lets them find something they're certain you'll appreciate.

Vacations. The Saver can be a major fun-killer on vacation. They can get so focused on how much things cost that they miss out on the fun of being together somewhere new. When you and your Saver plan a vacation, make sure the budget includes not just hotel and travel expenses, but incidentals like taxi fares, tips, and tickets for events and attractions. Leave some room for spontaneous fun, if possible. Savers hate money surprises, so the more prepared they are for the spending, the better.

If you can, plan for these money moments in advance to make sure you have some money set aside. The Saver is brilliant at finding ways to cut back in other areas to make room for spending in a specific category. Start early and let the Saver do what Savers do best.

The Spender

No one loves a money moment more than a Spender. If you're married to a Spender, be prepared for the rush of adrenaline they feel when money moments come along. Also prepare yourself for the anxiety and guilt Spenders can feel when they realize they've spent too much.

Here's how you can help your Spender keep an even keel during life's big money moments:

Holidays. Holidays are like Spender-palooza—it's the season for giving, and Spenders love to give. When Christmas lights start going up around town, I (Megan) watch Taylor's pupils turn into little cartoon dollar signs. He usually has a stash of gifts hidden in the back of our closet before I've finished cleaning up from Thanksgiving.

Contrary to popular assumptions, money moments can be stressful for Spenders too. They worry they'll run out of time to do all the shopping they hope to do. They get nervous about making sure they have just the right gift for everyone on their list. They can become obsessive about plans and details, running out at the last minute to replace all the silverware before the family arrives or grabbing one more last-minute present the day before Christmas.

Like the Saver, the Spender will find holidays a lot more manageable if they have a clear budget. Unlike the Saver, the Spender needs this budget to release their sense of guilt and keep them from ending up with too much debt when the bills come in.

Birthdays. Birthdays and anniversaries bring another chance for your Spender to shop for someone they love.

Again, the budget makes all the difference. In this case, you might need to take the lead. Give your Spender spouse a ballpark figure for gifts and parties. You could say, "Honey, I know your brother's birthday is coming up. I think we can throw a great party for under $500." Without some parameters, the Spender will be overwhelmed by the possibilities. Most Spenders are willing to stick with a budget they took part in creating, especially when they know they have their spouse's blessing to spend.

Vacation. Vacations are a Spender's paradise. When you travel, remember that the Spender will be ready to drop a little cash on every souvenir, attraction, and a six-dollar soda they can find. If there's a show in town, they'll want to see it. Some random attraction out by the interstate? Can't miss it. Countless little side trips will add up in a hurry if you don't set some limits ahead of time.

Spenders worry they are missing out on great experiences if they don't see everything there is to see while on vacation. To keep things in check, you need an itinerary that lines up with your budget. Do some research before you head out, scoping out all the options and identifying what you want to do and see. You won't be able to fit it all in, but the Spender can pick the most important places to visit and come to terms with missing a few stops.

The Security Seeker

The Security Seeker, like the Saver, can have a rough go of it during money moments. Unlike the Saver, the Security

Seeker is less concerned with the amount of money that's spent and more interested in where that money will come from. The Security Seeker's main worry in life is that there won't be enough money down the road. Since they usually don't have a target number for "enough," most Security Seekers live with a kind of low-grade stress throughout their adult lives. That stress can really spike during money moments as they watch what they fear is their life savings getting thrown out at the mall.

Here's how you can help your Security Seeker relax:

Holidays. Security Seekers do best when they have a lot of input in creating the holiday budget. Whereas Savers are looking to spend as little as possible, Security Seekers can be fine parting with lots of money as long as they know it's not going to make a dent in their future plans. That's why a well-defined budget is important, but not as important as the plan that will make that budget work. As the holidays get closer, work with your Security Seeker spouse to figure out where you can cut back to afford some holiday splurges. As the big event gets closer, remind your spouse that you've done the work to ensure all the fun is paid for responsibly.

Birthdays. Security Seekers aren't big fans of the splurge, but that doesn't mean they are reluctant gift givers. You can do a lot to ease your spouse's anxiety about birthdays by assuring them the birthday plans are concrete.

Vacations. As you and your Security Seeker spouse plan your vacation, make sure you're both very clear about where this money will come from. Will you need to take on a little extra credit card debt to cover the airfare? Do you need to tap into your savings to get the R & R you need? If so, how can you adjust your budget to get that money back in its proper place?

This can seem like a lot of work if you're not a Security Seeker, but a little effort on the front end of the vacation means a whole lot more enjoyment once you're there.

Security Seekers can seem unnecessarily anxious to the rest of us, but their fears come from the heart. They want to make sure their families are cared for down the road. The last thing they need is a spouse who tells them to stop worrying. Instead, help your partner focus on the present as well as the future. Remind them that the memories you make on vacation or during the holidays are an investment in the family too.

The Risk Taker

For Risk Takers, money moments are a time to get creative. Nothing makes a Risk Taker crabbier than being hemmed in by tradition. If you have a Risk Taker in your life, your biggest challenge will be giving them the leeway to be themselves in the middle of what can often be already chaotic situations.

Here's how to make the most of your Risk Taker's sense of adventure:

Holidays. Risk Takers love to think of new ways to celebrate the holidays. They're likely to suggest anything from having a taco bar for Christmas dinner to heading to Times Square for New Year's Eve. If you're married to a Risk Taker, be prepared to listen to some out-there ideas about gifts, food, travel, even holiday decorations. As outlandish as some of these thoughts may be, it's really important that you allow your spouse to feel heard.

If you're not a Risk Taker, it's easy to dismiss these crazy notions. Be as open as possible, and you might find a few ideas in there that will make life even more enjoyable for everyone. Is there really anything wrong with Christmas nachos?

Birthdays. Having a spouse who's a Risk Taker can be pretty great when your birthday rolls around. Your spouse's sense of adventure means you never know what your celebration will involve. If you worry that your husband or wife's spontaneity might get you both into financial trouble, be clear about these concerns well ahead of the actual event. The Risk Taker wants you to have a great time, and if they know spending too much will keep you from enjoying yourself, they'll likely be more than happy to find a way to have a blast on a budget.

Vacations. For a Risk Taker, a vacation isn't really a vacation unless there's some thrill involved, whether it's a trip to an unknown location or a day of walking city streets without a map. If your Risk Taker's ideas are going to break the bank, help them find ways to express their sense of adventure and creativity with more affordable options. What gets Risk Takers excited isn't how much something costs; it's the enticement of something new and different and unknown—and that doesn't have to cost anything extra. Challenge your Risk Taker to come up with inventive ideas on the cheap, and they'll rise to the occasion.

The Flyer

Since Flyers rarely think about money, they don't get stressed out about money moments. That said, they do get anxious about all the planning that goes along with vacations, birthdays, or holidays.

Here's how you can help your Flyer manage the stress of money moments:

Holidays. Because Flyers are not inclined to plan ahead, they are prone to last-minute impulse decisions that can lead to overspending and stress. Help your Flyer by talking about your holiday budget early on. Make sure to give them plenty of input on the budget; it's easy to become controlling with a Flyer, but that just leads to resentment down the road.

Talk about what kinds of gifts you'd like to get for the people on your list. If you're having guests, figure out what you'll feed them and map out a plan for getting everything ready on time. Having all the details put together in advance means less eleventh-hour impulse spending.

Birthdays. The Flyer is as likely to forget your birthday as they are to put together an over-the-top, thoughtful celebration. That means it helps to drop some hints as you lead up to a birthday. Remind your spouse that it's the thought that counts, not the last-minute purchase.

Vacations. Flyers like to be fairly spontaneous, so be ready for your vacation plans to morph a bit as you get ready to travel. Flyers are also more than willing to make sure everyone on the vacation gets some say in how you will spend your time, so talk about your expectations for what to see and do and where to stay.

Because they tend to be spontaneous and fairly stress-free, Flyers can add a needed bit of fun to every money moment. They are great at being present and can help everyone around them do the same.

ACKNOWLEDGMENTS

TO our dear friends Scott and Bethany Palmer: Thank you both for paving the way for such an incredible mission; for fulfilling your calling of spreading this message; and for being trusting enough to pass the torch on to us. We're grateful to continue this legacy, and we hope to make you proud.

To our Money Couple Team—Katelen, Kat, Claudia, and Evan: Each of you has put a tremendous amount of time and effort into this project, and we know this couldn't have been possible without you guys on board. Thank you for your creative input and for putting up with our crazy ideas.

Jeremiah 29:11

ABOUT THE AUTHORS

TAYLOR and **MEGAN KOVAR** recently took on the mantle of Scott and Bethany Palmer, the original Money Couple. The Kovars have been helping individuals and couples in their church and community to live healthier financial lives for years. Taylor guides many more through his company, Kovar Wealth Management. They live in Texas with their three lovely children, Kix, Kambry, and Kessly.

From the Publisher

GREAT BOOKS

ARE EVEN BETTER WHEN THEY'RE SHARED!

Help other readers find this one

- Post a review at your favorite online bookseller

- Post a picture on a social media account and share why you enjoyed it

- Send a note to a friend who would also love it—or better yet, give them a copy

Thanks for reading!